Behavior Management in the Middle School Classroom

A TEACHER'S GUIDE TO MEETING THE SPECIAL CHALLENGES OF EARLY ADOLESCENTS

Lee Canter and Marlene Canter

A PUBLICATION OF CANTER & ASSOCIATES, INC.

Editorial Staff
Carol Provisor
Barbara Schadlow
Kathy Winberry

Contributing Writer
Nancy-Jo Hereford

Design
Carol Provisor

©1995 Canter & Associates, Inc.
P.O. Box 2113, Santa Monica, CA 90407-2113
800-262-4347   310-395-3221

Library of Congress Catalog Card Number 95-078858
ISBN 1-57271-003-9

Printed in the United States of America
First printing August 1995
02 01 00 99 98 8 7 6 5 4 3

PD4111

CONTENTS

Introduction v

CHAPTER 1   Getting to Know the Students You Teach 1

CHAPTER 2   Meeting Discipline Challenges by Developing Your Strengths 11

CHAPTER 3   Meeting Discipline Challenges Using the Middle School Concept 21

CHAPTER 4   Creating Your Classroom Discipline Plan 33

CHAPTER 5   Putting Your Plan to Work in Your Classroom 53

CHAPTER 6   Getting Parents on Your Side 69

CHAPTER 7   Succeeding with Difficult Students 93

CHAPTER 8   Managing Homework Issues with Ease 121

CHAPTER 9   Accentuate the Positive! 139

INTRODUCTION

The Pivotal, Middle School Years

With all its challenges, middle school is one of the most exciting, most important areas of education to be involved in today.

More and more, researchers looking at the middle school are recognizing what a unique and pivotal time it is. In the past we've thought of early adolescents as junior versions of high school students—and that's what we called them. Not only was the junior high curriculum modeled after the high school, so was the structure of the school. Large, impersonal classes, 45-minute periods, and no "base"—save a locker in the hall—were the norm. If this environment wasn't conducive to learning and appropriate behavior from every student, conventional wisdom said the student needed to change, not the environment.

The "middle school movement" has turned that notion on its head. As a teacher of early adolescents, you are part of a groundbreaking effort to change the very structure of schooling at the middle level. Teachers like you are embracing new practices like teaming, flexible scheduling, and heterogeneous grouping. You are developing curriculum that addresses the questions and concerns of young adolescents. You are working with colleagues to create family-like units that help every student feel part of the enterprise of schooling. With each change, the goal is the same: to create an educational environment that meets the special needs of early adolescents.

What fuels this change? It is the growing understanding of the critical nature of the middle school years. This is the time when young people can make decisions that affect them for the rest of their lives—decisions about staying in school or starting on the road to dropping out; decisions about engaging in risky behaviors, such as drinking, using drugs, having sex. You know that early adolescents are testing boundaries and trying on independence. At the same time, they still need—and want—firm and caring guidance from adults to negotiate this difficult passage from childhood to later adolescence.

All these factors contribute to making teaching in the middle grades tougher than ever. Indeed, surveys show that discipline is among your number-one concerns. Far too many middle school teachers say they feel more like police officers than educators in their classrooms. And when you look for answers, all too often you struggle to find classroom-management materials tailored to the middle level.

Solutions for You and for Your Students

Behavior Management in the Middle School Classroom has been specially created to acknowledge the special needs of those "kids in the middle"—and of the teachers who work with them. The concepts and strategies that appear in this book have been tested and fine tuned for nearly two decades, giving you professional ability to make a lasting impact on your students at this critical juncture in their lives.

This comprehensive resource book draws on four Canter & Associates programs—Assertive Discipline®, Succeeding with Difficult Students®, How to Get Parents on Your Side®, and The High-Performing Teacher®—to create a middle school guide that offers you proven ideas and strategies to meet your most pressing needs: how to build a positive relationship with students; how to create a fair and consistent discipline plan; how to work with difficult students who constantly disrupt; how to get the support and involvement of parents.

As a middle school teacher, you know full well the ups and downs of this pivotal age. One day a 12-year-old has the sophistication of an adult; the next, the temperament of a young child. As the adults charged with caring for and educating these ever-vacillating child-adults, it can be a frustrating and overwhelming task at times. Yet, just as often, it's deeply satisfying—and even fun!

The strategies in *Behavior Management in the Middle School Classroom* are geared to help you rediscover the excitement and the rewards of working with early adolescents by letting you get back to doing what you do best—*teach*.

Getting to Know the Students You Teach

Robin Miller
Middle School Teacher
Newton, Massachusetts

*"When people find out I teach eighth-graders—
and that includes noneducators and teachers of
elementary or high school grades—they often ask
'How can you stand it?' Well, I can't think of
teaching any other age. Dull moments are rare,
and it's a wonderful challenge."*

They call them "the wonder years," and the wonder of it may be that early adolescents get through these years at all! This time marked by tremendous physical, social and emotional changes is one of the most significant and stressful in all of life. It is the time when children enter puberty and emerge looking—if not acting—like the adults they soon will be. It's a time of determining who one is and how one fits into a complex social world.

But it's also an intensely exciting time in a young person's life. There are new awakenings, new responsibilities, new freedoms to explore. Early adolescents begin to look at their world differently, to challenge ideas, to test the limits. While it's an unnerving and often frustrating time for those adults—parents and teachers—charged with guiding and educating these young people, dull moments *are* rare.

As a teacher of early adolescents, you know every one of these characteristics, and more. You know what it's like to ride the emotional roller-coaster called early adolescence, to try to teach young people who are up one moment and down the next, whose coping skills are still in low gear. But what's most important to recognize is the pivotal role you play in your students' lives. For underlying all of the facts and myths about this age is a critical truth—early adolescence is a turning point for every young person. It is the time when young adolescents can make fateful choices—in peer associations, in activities like drug and alcohol use or engaging in sexual behavior, in such decisions as applying oneself in school or moving toward dropping out—that can affect them the rest of their lives. As the 1989 Carnegie report on early adolescence, *Turning Points,* put it so well, "The period of life from ages 10 to 15 represents for many young people their last best chance to choose a path toward productive and fulfilling lives."

This book is designed to help you in guiding your students' behavior to enable them to make the choices that lead to healthy, fulfilling lives. Granted, the challenges are great, but the rewards can be even greater.

One message that will be oft repeated throughout this book is the importance of getting to know your students well. To be able to reach and influence a student, you must build a relationship with that young person. That process starts with understanding the needs and motivations of this age. Early adolescence is a unique time, and while every child who goes through it experiences it differently, there are commonalties.

This chapter explores those commonalties. Here you'll find a quick overview of the behaviors that are generally characteristic of this age. You'll also find very specific help in the form of student surveys to use in getting acquainted with your own students. Think of these surveys as a start at relationship building.

Not Just "Hormones with Feet"

Developmentally, early adolescence is often compared to infancy in terms of the tremendous scope of changes that occur in a relatively short period of time. The onset of puberty creates hormonal imbalances. Although the stereotyped view of young adolescents as "hormones with feet" is increasingly seen as exaggerated, these physical changes do make young adolescents moodier and more excitable than older or younger people—with obvious implications for behavior management.

Outward changes also create new kinds of inner feelings and new pressures to contend with. For girls, who tend to mature sexually about two years before boys, the onset of puberty often leads to an intense self-consciousness about and dissatisfaction with their bodies. Their earlier maturation also means they may be attracted to older boys, while not prepared for the sexual knowledge or aggressiveness of these more "mature" teens.

Although young adolescent boys may not have the body image problems that girls experience, the disparity in size between girls and boys can create general feelings of awkwardness in social interactions. Boys may become more self-conscious about muscle size and sports ability, as those issues take on new importance in the middle grades.

The Need to Fit In

The physical changes early adolescents experience and the young adolescent's increased focus on appearance lead inevitably to serious questions about what is normal and then: "Am I normal? Am I like everybody else? Do I fit in?" Young adolescents are intensely aware of their own selves and of others—perhaps more so than at any other time in life. As their understanding of the world increases, they want to find their place in it. That's why "personalizing" curriculum and connecting content to students' own interests, concerns and needs is so successful with this age.

The intense self-consciousness of early adolescence makes it a vulnerable time for self-esteem. Most kids this age—despite outward shows of bravado — suffer from a lowered self-esteem as they struggle with the confusion that comes with a changing physical self and a sense of uncertainly about who they are and where they fit in—not quite child anymore, but not adult either. Fortunately, as most young teens move through adolescence and begin to mature physically, socially and emotionally, their self-esteem returns to a more positive level.

But not for all—and especially not for students who are at risk and eventually drop out of school. For these kids, studies show, low self-esteem plagues them and influences their views of their place in key institutions like school. Dropouts generally don't feel good about themselves and don't think they fit in. Though adolescents may not be able to officially act on those feelings until high school, when they can legally drop out, feelings of alienation from school often take root in the vulnerable middle-grades years.

The need to "fit in" also means that early adolescents look increasingly to their peers for reassurance and acceptance. This is an age when sticking out and not looking, sounding or acting "right" are the greatest sins of all. Consequently, peer relationships can contribute to young adolescents' risky behavior, such as when they use drugs or alcohol to gain acceptance from peers.

A sense of belonging is acutely important at this age. It's that need which middle-level schools fill when they break up a grade level into smaller teams of students and teachers. Helping kids and teachers get to know one another well supports both early adolescents and behavior management, too.

Who's in Charge Here?

The penchant for questioning authority and testing its limits may be among the most frustrating characteristics of this age for teachers and parents alike. But it's perfectly normal. The need for greater independence and freedom to form one's own opinions and judgments is part of the movement toward adolescence. Early adolescents are learning—if slowly—to be more self-reliant and self-directed, though they still require and benefit from adult guidance in learning decision-making skills and how to make responsible choices in behavior. These stirrings of independent thought and action can, and often do, translate into contentious and uncooperative behavior.

Peer relationships also become more important as young adolescents assert their independence and move away from the authority of parents and teachers. The tendency of early adolescents to look to peers for approval also heightens the flaunting of traditional authority. As most middle grades teachers know all too well, 11-, 12-, 13- and 14-year-olds can be at their most annoying and difficult when they are part of a group.

But there's also good news from research in this area. Though young adolescents may debate and fuss over boundaries set for them, most don't stray that far from the values they were raised with. They are still emotionally dependent on their parents or other key adult figures in their lives and still look for and need support, encouragement and guidance. They want their parents' approval, and their teachers', too, if they have established a relationship with them.

The transition from dependence to independence for young people should be a gradual one. Parents in particular may misread their young adolescent children and think these adult-looking persons are ready for more adultlike choices and freedoms than they are. Reasonable behavior limits—whether set at home or as part of a structured discipline plan at school—can provide young teens with a degree of security in a turbulent time.

At Risk and In Need

The challenges that young adolescents face are so great, one wonders how so many youngsters manage to safely negotiate the twisting paths of this age and arrive at adulthood as basically normal and productive individuals. The most successful usually have an armor that serves as a strong defense—a supportive home environment. Research shows that a well-functioning family is one of the best predictors of kids who are able to move through adolescence remaining calm and healthy.

As a middle grades teacher today, you know that for more and more young adolescents, that armor is missing. The strife of divorce, separation, single parenthood and poverty in which many early adolescents live is compounded by the messages all but the most sheltered young teens are exposed to daily. Our society is more graphic and less inhibited than ever before about such issues as sexuality,

substance use and violence. At a time when young teens are trying on personalities, looking for the one that "fits," the images and messages they receive about what is acceptable behavior and what is "desirable" are often far more sophisticated than the emotions and reasoning skills with which they're operating. And out of that ignorance or naiveté, young adolescents can make poor choices that, tragically, can affect them for the rest of their lives.

The problem of kids at risk is real, and as a teacher in middle school or junior high, you know it better than any statistician. Yet, the statistics are compelling. The Carnegie Council on Adolescent Development estimates that of 28 million children between the ages of 10 and 17, seven million are highly vulnerable to school failure and high-risk behaviors—using tobacco, alcohol and illegal drugs; sexual activity, with its risks of AIDS, venereal disease and pregnancy; gang activity and use of weapons. That's one in four young people in this country today at great risk of living unhealthy, unproductive and perhaps unnaturally short lives. That's some of the students you teach.

Making a Difference

You can make a difference. This book will show you new ways and encourage you to find others to help students learn to choose healthy behaviors and start to shape productive lives. Nobody will say it's easy. You know that even those kids who come from balanced and supportive homes can be a trial at times. The really difficult students can be a nightmare. They disrupt your lessons and leave you disheartened and discouraged. They can make you wonder why you went into teaching at all. And sometimes, when their anger surges to a feverish pitch over the smallest of slights or frustrations, they can terrify you.

Even those kids can be reached. It doesn't happen overnight. It takes time, effort and genuine caring. And it doesn't happen without a willingness from *you* to understand the early adolescents you teach, to see each as a unique individual who's not quite formed and can still be molded, who beneath the outward flightiness or indifference or anger is a person working through a significant and critical passage in life, a person who needs your guidance and support as much as the knowledge you can impart.

Getting to Know Your Students

Starting on page 8 there are three ready-to-reproduce pages for getting to know each student better. You'll find a student survey, "Tell Me About You," that's helpful, especially at the start of the

---

What Kind of Teacher Do *You* Want?

Your opinions matter to me. So please answer these questions honestly.

Name (optional) _____ Date _____

Check the six qualities that are most important to you. Then put an X by the top three.

Middle school teachers should:

_____ be respectful of students.

_____ be willing to listen.

_____ be interested in what they teach.

_____ know a lot about what they teach.

_____ be interested in the world and know what interests middle school kids.

_____ have a sense of humor.

_____ be fun to be around.

_____ demonstrate warmth and kindness.

_____ be easy to talk to.

_____ be fair.

Please finish these sentences.

The best teacher I ever had _____
_____
_____
_____

The worst thing a teacher can do to me is_____
_____
_____
_____

Tell Me About *You*

Welcome to my class! Getting to know you is important to me, and your answers will help. Your responses will be kept private, so please be honest. If you need more room to answer, use another sheet of paper or the back of this page.

Teacher: _____ Date _____

NAME: _____ Grade & Class _____

Brothers and Sisters:

Name _____ Age _____

Name _____ Age _____

Name _____ Age _____

Special Friends: _____
_____

These are my favorite things to do:_____
_____

These are my favorites:

Book:_____ Singer or group: _____

Movie: _____ Song: _____

TV show:_____ Food: _____

Some of the things that bug me are:_____

I worry about: _____

School would be better if:_____

This is what a teacher did last year that I really liked:_____
_____

This is what a teacher did last year that bothered or upset me:_____
_____

One goal I'd like to accomplish this year:_____

---

year, for learning a little about each student's likes, dislikes, preferences and pet peeves. (Keep a record of the "likes" to refer to when choosing positive rewards for your discipline plan described in Chapter 4.)

For a helpful means of finding out what students are looking for from you, reproduce and share "What Kind of Teacher Do You Want?" on page 9. Consider giving this survey at the start of school and midyear, to see if students' views and preferences change. Comparing responses across grade levels can provide insights into how sixth-, seventh- and eighth-graders change in needs as they move through early adolescence—and what stays the same.

Use the "Tell Me About It" sheet on page 10 to invite students to share a concern or problem privately. Opening lines of communication is key to developing rapport with students and earning their trust. In the next chapter, we'll look at strategies for enhancing your own communication skills and strengthening your mission as a middle grades teacher.

TELL ME ABOUT IT…

Sometimes the best way to work through a problem is to share it with someone. If something's bothering you, tell me about it here. It's just between you and me.

Name _____ Grade & Class _____

_____
_____
_____
_____
_____
_____
_____
_____
_____
_____
_____
_____
_____
_____
_____

Sometimes just airing a problem helps you feel better. But if would you like to talk with me one-on-one about this problem, tell me when:

_____
_____

Do you think other kids have this same concern, or a similar one? Would this make a good problem to bring up in class (without naming names)? Tell me what you think:

_____
_____
_____

Tell Me About You

Welcome to my class! Getting to know you is important to me, and your answers will help. Your responses will be kept private, so please be honest. If you need more room to answer, use another sheet of paper or the back of this page.

Teacher: _____ Date _____

NAME: _____ Grade & Class _____

Brothers and Sisters:

Name _____ Age _____

Name _____ Age _____

Name _____ Age _____

Special Friends: _____

_____

_____

These are my favorite things to do: _____

_____

These are my favorites:

Book: _____ Singer or group: _____

Movie: _____ Song: _____

TV show: _____ Food: _____

Some of the things that bug me are: _____

_____

I worry about: _____

_____

School would be better if: _____

_____

This is what a teacher did last year that I really liked: _____

_____

This is what a teacher did last year that bothered or upset me: _____

_____

One goal I'd like to accomplish this year: _____

_____

What Kind of Teacher Do You Want?

Your opinions matter to me. So please answer these questions honestly.

Name (optional) _____ Date _____

**Check the six qualities that are most important to you.
Then put an X by the top three.**

Middle school teachers should:

_____ be respectful of students.

_____ be willing to listen.

_____ be interested in what they teach.

_____ know a lot about what they teach.

_____ be interested in the world and know what interests middle school kids.

_____ have a sense of humor.

_____ be fun to be around.

_____demonstrate warmth and kindness.

_____ be easy to talk to.

_____ be fair.

Please finish these sentences.

The best teacher I ever had _____

_____

_____

_____

The worst thing a teacher can do to me is _____

_____

_____

_____

TELL ME ABOUT IT...

Sometimes the best way to work through a problem is to share it with someone. If something's bothering you, tell me about it here. It's just between you and me.

Name _____ Grade & Class _____

_____

_____

_____

_____

_____

_____

_____

_____

_____

_____

_____

_____

_____

Sometimes just airing a problem helps you feel better. But if would you like to talk with me one-on-one about this problem, tell me when:

_____

_____

Do you think other kids have this same concern, or a similar one? Would this make a good problem to bring up in class (without naming names)? Tell me what you think:

_____

_____

_____

Meeting Discipline Challenges by Developing Your Strengths

Velvet McReynolds
Middle School Teacher
Birmingham, Alabama

"I have a personal mission statement, and it helps me remember that building relationships with students is my first priority. I can't teach if my students aren't with me."

Successful behavior management is not simply a matter of keeping the lid on disruptive behavior. It's also about changing students' attitudes and responses and helping them learn to make the right behavior choices. And that involves understanding the impact your own attitude and responses have on your students and the atmosphere in your classroom.

Think about you for a moment. Why do you teach in the middle grades? What's important to you, and what do you want to accomplish as a teacher? How do you communicate your priorities to students? Do kids really know what behavior is expected—and what's not acceptable—in your classroom?

Even if you think you have a good answer to each of those questions, read this chapter. It will show you how to develop a clear sense of mission—one that makes building relationships with students a priority. And it will enhance your ability to communicate with students in a positive, yet authoritative way. By developing these two key strengths—knowing what you're about as a teacher and how to make yourself understood to students—you'll increase your behavior-management skills as well.

The Power of Mission

Think back to your first day as a teacher in a middle school or junior high. What did you hope to accomplish? What ideals did you bring with you into the classroom? What was your mission—and is it still as clear to you today?

When teachers get frustrated and burned out, it's often because they've lost sight of their mission. Setting realistic goals for what you want to accomplish as a teacher, then putting those goals in the form of a mission statement, can go a long way

toward helping you feel successful as a teacher. It can help you keep the big picture in mind on days when riding the roller-coaster of early adolescence leaves your head spinning and your temper frayed.

If it has been a while since you really thought about why you teach, try this approach for sorting out what's important to you. Imagine that it's the night of your retirement dinner. The room is filled with former students. What would you want them to say about you? What kind of influence do you want to have on your students today that could stay with them for a lifetime?

Jot down some notes about what you would want to hear that night, on how you want your students to perceive you as a teacher. Then use those thoughts to create a mission statement.

Writing Your Mission Statement

A mission statement is a basic set of principles, a personal affirmation of your goals and objectives. It is a declaration of purpose, a blueprint for action.

What might one say? Here's how one seventh-grade teacher expresses her mission:

> *My mission as a teacher is to instill in my students a lifelong love of learning—to communicate to them that through learning they can make their dreams come true. I want to help all students believe in themselves, and through that belief, reach their highest potential.*

Here's how another middle school teacher defines his mission:

> *My mission is to build the self-esteem of my students and to help them become independent learners and responsible, self-disciplined individuals. I will respect my students' individual differences and will do everything I can to help them believe in themselves and develop their full potential. I will grow with my students as I continue to learn from them and from others in the field of education.*

Take your time in writing your mission statement. Remember, this is an expression of your basic direction as a teacher. Think about what you want to say, write down some ideas, then review your statement again in a day or two, to see if it really expresses your guiding vision as a teacher of early adolescents. Think about ways you can bring your own attitudes and actions in the classroom in harmony with your goals as a teacher. Continue to analyze and refine your mission statement until you are satisfied that it truly reflects the values that are most important to you as a middle grades teacher. As you develop your mission statement, you might draw on:

- the middle grades mission statements quoted above.

- reflections on teachers who were or are your role models—as a student and as an adult.

- your own reflections on what is most rewarding to you as a teacher, what's most frustrating, what gives you the greatest sense of satisfaction.

- your goals—personal and professional.

- your assessment of our own values, strengths, and priorities.

Refining Your Mission: Teaching Students, Not Subjects

If you reread the two mission statements on this and the previous page, you'll find a key ingredient in developing your strengths as a middle grades teacher. Did you notice that neither teacher talks about teaching subjects? Both statements focus on students—on developing the potential of individuals, not of a class. That's an important distinction.

Successful teachers recognize that they teach students, not English or math or science or art. They teach individuals, not six classes or five periods a day.

That's not to say content is unimportant or that your skill and expertise in your subject area are not part of what makes you a good teacher. But you also know that the best lesson in the world will fail if students are disruptive, disorganized, and not ready to learn. Building relationships with your students is fundamental to your success as an instructor and dispenser of knowledge. Starting each day with the goal of reaching individuals, not of getting through a lesson plan, will have a profound impact on how your students perceive you, and in turn, on the success and satisfaction you receive from teaching. Consider that difference carefully as you write your mission statement.

Living Your Mission

Once you're satisfied with your mission statement, record it on "The Power of Mission" sheet on page 19. Why write it down? Having a written statement encourages you to focus on your mission in ways that simply keeping it in mind doesn't. Tuck your mission statement inside your plan book, frame it for your desk, or post it in your office or bedroom at home. You'll find that this constant reminder of what you're about as a teacher will help you be the best teacher you can be. If you see before you the

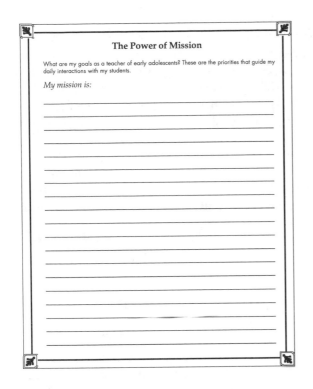

The Power of Mission

What are my goals as a teacher of early adolescents? These are the priorities that guide my daily interactions with my students.

My mission is:

goal of "raising my students' self-esteem and treating them with respect and dignity" every day, you will more consciously seek ways to build relationships with students and give that extra one-on-one attention when it's needed.

Think of your mission statement as a personal accountability tool. At the end of each day, take a minute to review the ways in which you met—or moved closer to meeting—your personal goals. That simple exercise will leave you feeling more positive about yourself and your students.

The Power of Communication

Your mission statement is like a compass. It steers you in the direction of effective teaching. But it's not a magic wand. It's not enough to say you want to "build positive relationships with students." How you respond to students sets the tone for your classroom.

Teachers who demonstrate by their actions that they are open and interested in students are better able to establish rapport with them and create a positive classroom climate. Developing effective communication skills involves evaluating your response style and using techniques that enhance your interactions with students.

Response Styles: Reactive or Proactive

From years of working with educators and watching them work with students, we've identified three types of responses that teachers consistently use in dealing with student behavior. Two of those—nonassertive and hostile styles—are basically reactive in nature. The teacher reacts to disruptive or noncompliant behavior. The third—the assertive response style—is proactive and reflects a teacher's commitment to teaching students to choose appropriate, responsible behavior.

Not surprisingly, the assertive style is the most effective. To help you evaluate your own response style—and help you develop the qualities of an assertive style—let's look first at characteristics of the more ineffective styles.

Nonassertive Response Style

A teacher who is basically nonassertive does not communicate his or her behavior expectations to students in clear and unquestionable terms. Instead, nonassertive teachers are inconsistent in how they respond to inappropriate behavior. One day they may allow students to disrupt without responding at all. The next day they may react firmly, demanding that students stop the same misbehavior. Such responses leave students confused—and often eager to challenge—because they don't know what to expect.

Teachers who respond nonassertively to students communicate that they are unsure of themselves and their abilities. They appear *powerless*. This response style often results in a classroom environment in which there is constant testing of wills between teacher and students.

Hostile Response Style

A teacher who uses iron-fisted discipline and puts students down may control his or her classroom, but at the expense of students' self-esteem. Teachers who respond to students' behavior in a hostile manner send the message to students that "I don't like you" or "There is something wrong with you." They use discipline to control students or to get back at them, rather than to teach them how to behave.

Hostile teachers often view the classroom as a battleground. They have negative expectations of their ability to deal with students, and they blame the students, the parents, and the administration for their problems.

The Value of an Assertive Response Style

An assertive response style is one in which the teacher clearly, confidently, and consistently states his or her expectations to students, and is prepared to back up these words with actions. When teachers respond assertively, they communicate to students exactly what behavior is acceptable and what is not, what will happen when the student chooses to behave, and what will happen when the student chooses not to behave. There is no room for confusion.

However, assertive teachers have positive expectations of their ability to motivate students and communicate that attitude through their words and actions. They recognize an early adolescent's need for limits and are prepared to set those limits. At the same time, they recognize the vulnerable nature of the young adolescent and the need for warmth and encouragement. They acknowledge *appropriate* behavior as consistently as they discourage inappropriate conduct.

A teacher who responds assertively to students creates an atmosphere in which both the teacher and students have an opportunity to get their needs met. There is a balance established between the rights of the teacher and those of the students; between firm limits and warmth and support.

Students learn to trust and respect an assertive teacher. They clearly know the boundaries of acceptable and unacceptable behavior; thus, they have the opportunity to choose how they want to behave.

Acquiring the Posture of Assertive Teachers

What does an assertive response style look like in the classroom? Refer to the box on page 17 for three examples of how an assertive teacher responds to typical classroom situations. You'll also continue to find examples and guidance in developing an assertive response style throughout this book.

Start today to really listen to your own responses to students and to honestly reflect on whether you are responding in a positive, assertive style or a more reactive one. Keep in mind that no teacher responds consistently in the same way. On a good day, when you are feeling confident, you may respond more assertively than on a bad day, when nonassertive or even hostile responses may creep into your interactions with students. However, by learning to recognize reactive responses, you'll be better able to shift to more proactive, positive approaches to communicating with students.

Effective behavior management does begin with you. But it need not be you alone. In restructured middle schools, teachers are finding new strength and support among team members, particularly when they discipline as a team. In the next chapter, we'll look at how teachers of early adolescents can make the most of the "middle school concept" to encourage more consistent and successful behavior management.

How Would You Respond?

Here are three problem scenarios and assertive responses. Try covering up the "response" paragraph and formulating your own intuitive response to each situation. Then compare your response to the assertive response that follows.

Situation #1: A seventh-grade teacher is standing at the front of the room giving a lecture. As he speaks, he notices a few students in the back of the room are looking out the window or doodling. They aren't bothering anyone, but they aren't paying attention either. It's easy to ignore this type of behavior, but the assertive teacher won't.

THE ASSERTIVE RESPONSE: While continuing to lecture, the teacher walks to the back of the room and stands near those students who are off task. He doesn't stop the lesson, but his close presence nudges the off-task students back on task.

KEY POINTS TO REMEMBER: Assertive teachers firmly let students know— through their verbal directions and through their body language—what is expected of them, but they do so in ways that allow them to teach, let other students learn, and preserve the self-respect of the problem students.

Situation #2: A belligerent sixth-grader is provoking other students around her. The teacher tells her to stop bothering her classmates and get to work. The student responds: "I don't want to."

THE ASSERTIVE RESPONSE: The teacher calmly gives the student a response from her classroom discipline plan. "Holly, that's one minute after class." The student responds, "Big deal." The teacher then walks over to Holly and calmly says, "Let's go outside." Once outside the classroom, she continues: "Holly, you have a choice. You can either settle down and get to work now or go to the office with me and call your mother. I cannot allow you to act this way in class."

KEY POINTS TO REMEMBER: The teacher de-escalates the situation in a calm, firm manner. By removing Holly from the classroom, she removes her from her audience—her peers—and gets her complete attention, while also preserving her self-respect by not embarrassing her in any way in front of her peers. The teacher's response can leave no doubt in the student's mind about what she wants her to do.

Situation #3: An eighth-grader who is quite immature for his age and has a great deal of difficulty staying on task is having a really good day. The student is working well in a cooperative learning group. He's on task, not bothering others, and contributing to the assignment.

THE ASSERTIVE RESPONSE: Assertive teachers also notice when students are behaving appropriately. In this situation, the teacher catches the student's eye, smiles, and gives a nod of recognition. Later, as the class is being dismissed, she speaks quietly to him: "You did a wonderful job working with your group today. Your contribution helped everyone finish on time."

KEY POINTS TO REMEMBER: The teacher acknowledges the student's appropriate behavior, thereby encouraging him to repeat it, but in a way that doesn't embarrass him in front of his peers.

Velvet McReynolds on Living Your Mission

I have a personal mission statement. In it, I state that "building relationships with students" is my first priority. I can't teach if my students aren't with me.

What's key in building relationships with early adolescents? I've always had a way with this age. Even as a young teacher I was able to understand my students and to be understood by them. Then, I intuitively did things that helped my students trust and respect me. Over time I've come to recognize the effectiveness of those actions and responses, and today I do them more consciously.

- I listen.

- I try to "hear between the lines."

- I look students in the eye.

- I observe and validate.

- I smile.

- I speak respectfully to every student, every day.

- I make a point of talking to each of my students on a personal level every day.

- I use gentle touches—on the shoulder, arm.

- I'm at the door when they arrive and up when they leave. I move purposefully around the room throughout the class. I'm not a desk sitter.

I want students to feel that I'm approachable. I encourage them to share with me through journal writing. And I respond, be it in the journal or in a private conversation. I get to know my students, so that I can get to the heart of what's eating them when they act out in my classroom.

There is a direct relationship between my behavior and my students' behavior. The foremost component of building a relationship with early adolescents is showing them respect.

Velvet McReynolds has taught English/language arts in grades 6–8 for 21 years, most of that time in Los Angeles schools. Currently she teaches at Simmons Middle School in Birmingham, Alabama. McReynolds is one of six outstanding teachers profiled in Lee Canter's program The High-Performing Teacher.

The Power of Mission

What are my goals as a teacher of early adolescents? These are the priorities that guide my daily interactions with my students.

My mission is:

_____

_____

_____

_____

_____

_____

_____

_____

_____

_____

_____

_____

_____

_____

_____

_____

Meeting Discipline Challenges Using the Middle School Concept

Julie Elliott
Middle School Principal
San Diego, California

"Teachers have to be empowered to control the behavior in their classrooms. When you have a schoolwide discipline plan, you take discipline away as an issue. If my rules are the same as your rules, then when students move from me to you, discipline is not an issue anymore. It's just consistency."

In the previous chapters, we've talked about some of the discipline challenges that middle-level teachers face in working with early adolescents. Without question, behavior management issues take up more of a teacher's time and energy today than in the past.

If, however, like more and more middle-level teachers, you are teaching in a middle school that has embraced many of the characteristics of the "middle school concept," you also have new relationships with colleagues in the form of teaming and new opportunities for building relationships with students that support and facilitate behavior management in important ways.

This chapter explores behavior management issues as they relate to changes in restructured middle schools. You'll find help in disciplining as a team and managing cooperative-group activities. The changes that restructuring brings also promote opportunities to look broadly at behavior policies that influence a school's overall climate, so the chapter winds up by exploring the value of implementing a schoolwide discipline plan.

The Team Approach to Behavior Management

If you teach in a middle school, chances are you're part of an interdisciplinary team. Teaming is one of the key features of the middle school concept, and it can have a very positive influence on student behavior.

In a large school, early adolescents can feel lost and overwhelmed. When students are interacting with hundreds of peers, up to a dozen different teachers and staff persons, and moving throughout a large building, there are often few opportunities for real attachments to develop but many opportunities for kids to get into trouble. Students who don't feel a strong sense of belonging, who don't experience consistency from one teacher to the next, and who aren't known as individuals to their teachers are more likely to be disruptive, in the classroom and in the halls.

On the other hand, when schools form small units or teams of students who share a core of teachers, attend classes with basically the same group of kids, and spend most or all of their time on one floor or wing of a building, they help to create an environment that is more nurturing, more structured, and more comfortable for early adolescents. Used effectively, teaming promotes a sense of community, where students feel they have a place and fit in. That atmosphere gives teachers a head start in helping students choose behaviors that enable this community of learners to thrive.

Building on Teaming: Establishing Consistency

To take advantage of the positive influence teaming can have on behavior management, begin by focusing on students' behavior as an important element of team planning and discussion. In fact, for some teams just starting out who don't feel ready to tackle interdisciplinary units, focusing on working together to address the behavior problems and needs of individual students is a comfortable way to start pooling ideas and coordinating your efforts as a team.

Here are ways to build on teaming to ease behavior management:

Set consistent rules.

It's just common sense that students are going to be better behaved when they have one set of rules to learn, rather than a set for each teacher. As well, for teams who teach together for some portion of the day, it's imperative that team members be of one mind when it comes to discipline. In Chapter 4, we detail how to set up a classroom discipline plan. For middle-level teachers, perhaps it should be thought of as a "team discipline plan."

When students know what the rules are, what the rewards are for following those rules, and what the consequences are for not following the rules, they know what behavior is acceptable and what is not. When all of the teachers in a team follow the same plan, there is no place for argument that "Mr. Green lets us do this . . ." or "Ms. White lets us do that . . ." Students cannot pit one teacher's rules against another or plead confusion or forgetfulness. The rules are the same in every class. Perhaps the rewards may vary, depending on the personality of the teacher, but the consequences should be the same, so that students know that choosing to misbehave in Ms. White's presence will have the same result as doing so in Mr. Green's.

Discipline as a team.

While consistent rules can help to decrease behavior problems, a cohesive team can more effectively address the problems and needs of students who don't follow those rules.

Set aside time during team meetings to discuss behavior issues. Brainstorm ways the team can work together to support those students who consistently act out and to provide them with the extra assistance or attention needed to help them make more responsible behavior choices.

In Chapter 7, you'll find guidance in developing an individualized behavior plan for difficult students. It's critical that all members of the team follow the plan. Showing consistency and solidarity as a team will demonstrate to difficult students that the team has their best interests at heart—and that you mean business!

Meet with parents as a team, too. You'll find that discipline conferences will be more productive when parents and all of a student's teachers are hearing the same information and responses. The plans that you develop will be done in concert with all of the key adults who can most directly impact a student's behavior.

However, do recognize that parents can feel overwhelmed and outnumbered in such a situation. Some teams find it helpful to include an administrator or a non-team teacher in the meeting, who moderates and ensures the parent maintains an equal voice in the discussion.

Negotiating Team Differences

How does a team arrive at consistent rules? And how do team members work through differences in discipline styles? Differences in style are often at root differences in attitude—seeing the classroom in the negative light of a battleground rather than with the positive view that all students can learn to behave appropriately. Use the strategies in Chapter 2 to help you and your colleagues focus on your mission as teachers of early adolescents and develop a discipline style that encourages positive interactions among students and teachers. You'll also find help in developing a plan that takes a positive approach to discipline in Chapter 4.

Sit down as a team and decide what basic rules are needed based on your particular population of students. Then decide together if each rule is reasonable and enforceable. Keep in mind that the most effective rules are those that are not ambiguous. They tell exactly what behavior is expected—*Don't interrupt when someone else is speaking; Be in your seat when the bell rings; Keep hands and feet to yourself*—and they don't leave room for interpretation.

Remember that the ability of your team to model cooperation and negotiating skills encourages students to imitate the same in their own group activities. Early adolescents need to see adults working together and compromising on their differences to reach a consensus. The cohesiveness of your team will do as much to encourage cooperative behavior among students as will the rules you agree on.

Managing Cooperative-Group Activities

More and more research shows conclusively the social and educational inequities that are fueled by tracking. Consequently, more and more schools—particularly middle schools—are moving to mixed-ability grouping. For many teachers, the most effective way to teach to the range of abilities in a heterogeneously grouped classroom is through cooperative-learning techniques.

If managed properly, cooperative-learning groups can help to decrease discipline problems in a classroom, because students have more opportunities to get to know one another and learn how to get along. When students in a group are responsible for one another's learning and for ensuring that every member achieves the group's goals, all students gain—whatever their ability.

However, it is also true that you can't simply throw a group of middle-schoolers together and expect them to cooperate and stay on task. If not properly managed, a group activity becomes a social affair—or a source of conflict when kids disagree over how to accomplish the assigned task. But by learning how to manage cooperative groups effectively, you can reap both the academic and the behavioral benefits of this teaching approach.

Teaching Cooperation as a Skill

The mistake that teachers often make in using cooperative-group activities is assuming students automatically know how to work as a team. Cooperation is a skill, and one that students will need all through life. Start now to help your students learn how to cooperate.

Begin by talking about what it means to cooperate. Draw on students' own experiences as members of sport teams or other groups to get a sense of what they recognize as the dynamics of cooperation. Talk about what a team is and what makes one work.

Then help students transfer team experiences in sports or clubs to working as a team in the classroom. Discuss the necessity of learning to share resources, time and ideas; learning to take turns in speaking and acting as group leader; and learning to respect others' ideas and views that are different from one's own. (You'll find more help in teaching cooperative-group skills in the section on "Teaching Responsible Behavior" in Chapter 5.)

Review these skills frequently as students work in groups. Conclude activities by discussing the challenges of working as a team and ask students to evaluate how well their groups work together. Does the group have trouble staying on task? Do members have trouble negotiating their differences?

Some teachers find that asking students to critique their group experiences in a journal helps students to focus on the accomplishments of the group and identify problems in working as a team. By helping students to identify the causes of fights and conflict among group members, you'll improve group behavior and productivity in future activities. Share the reproducible sheet, "How Well Do We Work Together," on page 30 for this purpose. Encourage

How Well Do We WORK TOGETHER?

Learning to cooperate and work with others on a team is an important skill. It's one you need today in the classroom and in sports. It's also a skill you'll need to be a valuable employee when you have a job. Use this page to help you reflect on how well you work as part of a team and how well your team works together. Please do not name names (except your own). Refer to I, we, or the group only.

Name (optional): _____ Date: _____

The group assignment: _____

This is what we accomplished as a group: _____

This is what I contributed to the group: _____

These are some of the problems I think our group has in working together: _____

Our group could have worked together more cooperatively by _____

I could have been a more valuable member of our group by _____

My goal for the next cooperative-group activity is _____

students not to point fingers but to focus on *I, we,* and *the group.* Ask group members to share their responses with one another and to discuss ways they can work together more equitably or effectively next time. Reading students' response sheets will help you gauge how you can help each team and the class as a whole interact more successfully for cooperative activities.

Identifying Roles and Rules for Group Members

One of the defining characteristics of cooperative learning is that each group member has a specific role and responsibility to fulfill in completing the task. By making the group responsible for one another's learning, you build on the strength of positive peer pressure: If a team of students know they all fail if Mark fails, they'll work harder to keep Mark on task—and discourage his tendency to act out and behave inappropriately.

Don't leave assigning roles to chance. Make it a first step in any group activity. By assigning every member a job, no one has any excuse to goof off or engage in disruptive behavior. They all have something to do!

Group members' roles may vary depending on the activity. Here are some to consider:

- The Manager or Leader keeps the group on task and makes sure each person is contributing.

- The Organizer gathers materials or resources the group will need.

- The Questioner analyzes the quality of the group's thinking, moderates when needed to be sure each member's ideas are being heard and makes sure all ideas have been explored.

- The Editor records the group's responses and creates a final draft of any written assignment.

- The Reporter presents to the rest of the class when necessary.

Share the reproducible sheet, "Getting Organized as a Group," on page 31 to help each group organize itself for a cooperative activity. It asks students to identify the role and responsibility of each member, to outline the task at hand and to consider rules the group may want to set for its members to help ensure a successful effort. Refer to the sheet as a checkpoint if group behavior seems to be wandering off task.

Getting Organized AS A GROUP

This sheet is designed to help you think through today's assignment and how you can complete it successfully by working together as a cooperative group. Please fill this sheet before you begin the assignment.

Date:_____ Class:_____

Our group assignment:_____

Roles and responsibilities

STUDENT	ROLE	RESPONSIBILITY
	Manager	
	Organizer	
	Questioner	
	Editor	
	Reporter	

Rules

Based on our experiences working together in the past, what rules—in addition to the classroom rules—will help us work together more cooperatively today?

Your Role in Keeping Students on Task

Your presence and participation in group work also is vital to keeping students on track. Start by setting rules for cooperative-group activities and reminding students of those rules before beginning an assignment. Here are four rules to consider:

- *Move quickly and quietly to your team.*

- *When in your team, discuss only the assignment.*

- *All members participate.*

- *If you need help, raise your hand.*

You'll also want to set clear rules for participation within the group. The purpose of those rules should be to help guide students in working cooperatively. For example:

- *Listen to each other.*
- *Only one person speaks at a time.*
- *No interrupting.*
- *No put-downs.*
- *All ideas get to be heard.*

Once students are in their groups, circulate from group to group. Check to be sure everyone understands the assignment and can get started. Praise evidence of cooperation you observe: "Good job dividing up the parts of this problem among the team!" Or you may see an opportunity to guide students in understanding how to work more effectively as a team: "That's a good start, but let's think about how you can break this problem apart, so that each team member tackles one part of it."

As you work with one group, scan the room to check for signs of groups that are getting off track. Use eye contact to redirect group members, or move immediately to deal with disruptive behavior in one group that can get the entire class off task. (You'll find specific techniques for responding to disruptive behavior in Chapter 5.) Keep in mind that you need to continually monitor learning groups and provide praise, redirection, and if necessary, consequences.

Finally, evaluate each group assignment you give, to be sure that students truly gain from the opportunity for group thinking and interaction. If most students can just as easily do an activity on their own, it's probably not an effective group activity, and students may be more tempted to wander off task.

Supporting Restructuring with a Schoolwide Discipline Plan

While you're rethinking a school's organization, instruction and teaching methods, it just makes sense to rethink discipline, too. A restructuring movement can be the perfect time to institute more successful behavior-management strategies. One of the most effective systems at any level, but particularly in the middle grades when students benefit greatly from consistency, is a schoolwide discipline plan.

What is a schoolwide discipline plan? Basically, it is a plan that every staff member and student in the school follows. It means that not only are the rules the same from classroom to classroom, there are consistent rules for the common areas around the school. The rules posted in the halls, in the cafeteria, in the library, in every classroom apply to everyone. It means that every teacher and every support person is empowered to enforce those rules. It means that every student knows what behavior is acceptable and what is not at all times during the school day. A schoolwide discipline plan eliminates questions or confusion about rules and behavior expectations.

Using Team Discipline to Build School Discipline

Naturally, the path to creating a schoolwide discipline plan is made easier when you have an administrator at the helm who recognizes its value and finds the time and funds for training. (See the profile, page 29, of a middle school principal who makes the case for a schoolwide discipline plan.)

However, by following the ideas presented earlier in this chapter for disciplining as a team—as well as those in the next chapter for developing a classroom discipline plan—you have a powerful means of demonstrating the value of providing early adolescents with consistent rules, rewards and consequences.

Build a case to present to your principal and fellow teachers by having each team member keep a behavior tracking sheet (see the reproducible sheet in Chapter 4 on page 50) so that you can document decreases in disruptive behavior over time. As well, keep anecdotal records of improvement in difficult students' behavior and attitude. There's value in consistency. Your records will demonstrate it—and help every team member feel proud of your successes with the students on your team.

Julie Elliott on the Power of a Schoolwide Discipline Plan

Not long ago the California state attorney general used Horace Mann Middle School as a forum for a school safety media event. He selected our school by asking school security officials what school *ought* to be complete chaos; what school *should be* a gang-infested, weapons-run, terrible place—and *isn't*. They all said Horace Mann.

The challenges are great. We have nearly 2,000 sixth-, seventh- and eighth-graders who speak more than 30 languages. We're located in the most poverty-stricken zip code in the county and in the area with the highest crime rate. Our students come from socioeconomic levels that range from extreme poverty to middle class. Students represent ability levels that range from pre-literate and pre-verbal to highly gifted kids who read at the college level.

Our biggest problems have always been in maintaining discipline and behavior management. Eight years ago, before Horace Mann restructured to a middle school, there were major race-related fights on campus. We also were seeing some gang activity—Bloods and Crips wannabees.

The turnaround started with restructuring.

The ninth-graders moved out and the sixth-graders moved in. And with this change came a greater emphasis on creating a warm, nurturing, supportive environment for students. The principal before me started the process. She interviewed every staff member, looking for intelligent adults who truly believe that all children can learn and who take the time to build relationships with their students.

It was during that restructuring that I came to the school as a vice principal. Fours years ago I took over as principal, and what we also found is that a supportive environment alone isn't enough to maintain discipline. We still had big problems with students who were out of control. With only three administrators, I knew that I couldn't control

behavior. *Behavior management has to start in the classroom.* We wanted a plan that was positive, that emphasized rewards for good behavior rather than punishments for bad. That's the philosophy of Lee Canter's Assertive Discipline.

A schoolwide discipline plan frees teachers to do wonderful, creative things in their classrooms because the students know the rules, the positives and the consequences. There's no question about what behavior is allowed in this class or in this setting. With a positive behavior plan firmly in place, that teacher will maintain control.

We keep a tight rein. And the kids like it.

We've structured ourselves around order and around placing students in small groups within this huge school. We have teams at each level. Students at each level have the same core group of teachers, and they know that each teacher talks to every other teacher on the team. When there's a parent conference, it's with all four teachers. Students also have the same teacher advisor, resource specialist, and counselor for all three years.

Today we have a calm, well-functioning campus, and we've achieved it by working at several levels. You have to create a supportive environment for students *and* set clear and consistent rules for behavior. We don't "punish" anyone—that's not part of the lexicon of this school. It's rewards and delineated consequences. And one of the benefits of creating an atmosphere that's positive and loving is that everyone in the school looks more positively at their jobs—as teachers or learners.

Julie Elliott is principal of Horace Mann Middle School in San Diego, California. She was a middle school teacher for 12 years before coming to Mann.

How Well Do We WORK TOGETHER?

Learning to cooperate and work with others on a team is an important skill. It's one you need today in the classroom and in sports. It's also a skill you'll need to be a valuable employee when you have a job. Use this page to help you reflect on how well you work as part of a team and how well your team works together. Please do not name names (except your own). Refer to I, we, or the group only.

Name (optional): _____ Date: _____

The group assignment: _____
_____
_____

This is what we accomplished as a group: _____
_____
_____

This is what I contributed to the group: _____
_____
_____

These are some of the problems I think our group has in working together: _____
_____
_____

Our group could have worked together more cooperatively by _____
_____
_____

I could have been a more valuable member of our group by _____
_____
_____

My goal for the next cooperative-group activity is _____
_____
_____

Getting Organized AS A GROUP

This sheet is designed to help you think through today's assignment and how you can complete it successfully by working together as a cooperative group. Please fill this sheet out before you begin the assignment.

Date: _____ Class: _____

Our group assignment: _____
_____
_____

Roles and responsibilities

STUDENT	ROLE	RESPONSIBILITY
_____	Manager	_____
_____	Organizer	_____
_____	Questioner	_____
_____	Editor	_____
_____	Reporter	_____

Rules

Based on our experiences working together in the past, what rules—in addition to the classroom rules—will help us work together more cooperatively today?

_____
_____
_____
_____
_____
_____
_____
_____

CHAPTER 4

Creating Your
Classroom Discipline Plan

Marianne Herndon
Middle School Teacher
Humboldt, Tennessee

*"Lee Canter's Assertive Discipline plan
is the most helpful, the most effective
and the most practical. It transformed
my classroom. I don't know how I ever
got along without it."*

nderstanding the students you teach, developing your own strengths as a middle-level teacher, and drawing on the support of the colleagues with whom you team are all key to promoting positive behavior management and feeling in control in your classroom. But nothing replaces the power of having a classroom discipline plan—a set of rules, rewards and consequences that applies to every student in every class. Because you have a system that lets you spell out the behaviors you expect from students and what they can expect from you, it will give you greater confidence in managing the often challenging and unruly behavior of early adolescents.

Planning: The Key to Successful Classroom Management

When you have a plan for how you will respond to student behavior, you don't have to make on-the-spot decisions about what to do when a student misbehaves—or how to properly recognize a student who behaves appropriately. You know what behavior you expect in the classroom and how you will respond to its presence or absence, your students know what to expect, and, perhaps most important, guesswork and stress are eliminated from your daily disciplinary efforts.

A discipline plan also protects students' rights. It helps ensure that you deal with each student in a fair and consistent manner. And it protects your rights as a teacher to *teach*.

Three Key Components in Your Classroom Discipline Plan

A classroom discipline plan has three parts:

1. **Rules** that students must follow at all times.

2. **Positive recognition** that students receive for following the rules.

3. **Consequences** that result when students choose not to follow the rules.

This chapter outlines how to create your classroom discipline plan. You'll find help with setting rules, developing positive rewards for students who follow the rules and establishing graduated consequences for students who break those rules.

In the previous chapter, we discussed the value of setting rules and consequences that are followed by all of the teachers in an interdisciplinary team. Although we speak in terms of creating a "classroom discipline plan" throughout this chapter, for those teachers working in teams, use the guidelines in this chapter to develop a discipline plan that will be consistent from classroom to classroom. You'll find your plan will be more successful when it's adopted by all of the teachers in your team.

Creating Your Classroom Discipline Plan: Setting Rules

To successfully manage your classroom, you have to know how you want students to behave. You need to be very clear about your expectations and communicate those expectations to students. That's what setting behavior rules is all about.

The Value of Rules for Early Adolescents

Once students emerge from the elementary years, many middle-level teachers make the mistake of assuming kids are "old enough to know how to behave." Yet observation and common sense tell us that's not true. As we discussed in Chapter 1, early adolescents need the security of behavior boundaries. At a confusing time in their lives, they benefit from having fair and consistent limits on behavior. Your classroom rules tell students what is acceptable behavior and what is not.

In addition, many young people today come from homes where parents themselves are poor role models for behavior, where behavior expectations are undefined and rules are either not stated or not enforced. These students, as well as kids from more stable homes, are also bombarded by media images of guns, sex and violence; of celebrities whose behavior spans from irresponsible to downright dangerous. Young adolescents are very vulnerable to imitating such behavior. More than ever today, they need the structure and guidance that your classroom rules provide.

Guidelines for Setting Rules

There's an art and a science to setting effective behavior rules. Here are some guidelines.

Behavior rules must be observable.

Effective rules address behaviors you can objectively see or hear. For example:

- **Follow directions.**
- **Be in your seat when the bell rings.**
- **Don't interrupt when someone else is talking.**
- **No fighting, swearing or teasing.**

Now contrast those rules with these:

- Show respect for others.
- No fooling around.
- No unnecessary talking.

Notice how the first set of rules focuses on clearly defined behaviors. If the rule is to be in your seat when the bell rings, and students are still wandering around, there is no room for argument. The rule has been broken.

On the other hand, "showing respect," "fooling around," and "unnecessary talking" are vague directives and increase the possibility that students can argue with your judgment. What you consider to be disrespectful your students may not. And chatty early adolescents are sure to have a different opinion from yours of what is "unnecessary" conversation.

The point is this: **Don't let your rules put you in a position where students can argue with you.** Base your rules on clearly observable behaviors so that if a student breaks a rule, there is no room for argument.

Rules should be enforceable at all times in the classroom.

Think through a rule to be sure there are no logical and legitimate exceptions to it. For your classroom rules to have meaning and carry weight with students, they must be in force at all times. If you find yourself making exceptions to your classroom rules, their effectiveness will be greatly diminished.

Here are two examples of rules to avoid precisely because they cannot always be enforced.

- *Raise your hand and wait to be called on before you speak during class.* This rule sounds sensible, but there may be times when you want students to feel free to call out answers. This rule also won't work when using a cooperative-group activity during class. Then students need to be able to speak and discuss freely. **Your classroom rules should apply under all circumstances.**

- *Complete all homework assignments.* Again, this rule sounds very sensible, but it really does not relate to classroom behavior. And there may be times when students are unable to complete an assignment for legitimate reasons. **Classroom rules should be designed to guide students toward appropriate classroom behavior.** (For help in managing homework problems, see Chapter 8.)

Limit your rules to a few simple ones.

Your classroom rules should address behaviors that directly affect your ability to teach and students' ability to learn. For example, "Follow directions" is essential. You cannot teach if students don't follow your directives. "No fighting, swearing or teasing" sets a tone—that civilized behavior and the civil rights of all individuals in the classroom are to be upheld.

However, a laundry list of rules in which you try to cover every conceivable infraction or annoyance can be hard for students to remember and sends the message that you have little faith in their ability to control their own behavior. When there's a rule for everything, some kids are more tempted to test the rules.

Set rules that are appropriate for your students.

The rules that you devise for your classroom or that your team develops together must be appropriate to the needs of your students and your teaching style(s). Certainly, follow guidelines such as those presented here, but don't adopt a rule because it was suggested in a book or by a colleague. It has to be a rule that works for you, that you believe in, and that you are comfortable enforcing.

Involve students in setting classroom rules.

By asking students to help set classroom rules, you give them ownership over those rules and greater responsibility for ensuring that they and their classmates respect the rules. Involving students in setting classroom rules can get their buy-in to your

discipline plan and capitalize on positive peer pressure. And as teachers often find, students can be much tougher on one another than you are!

Turn to the "Classroom Rules Worksheet" on page 46 and use it to identify rules for your classroom discipline plan. Think through each rule and analyze it to be sure it is one that clearly defines a behavior expectation that is important to you and will positively affect the climate of your classroom. Return to the sheet and review your rules to be sure they are observable and can be enforced at all times, under all scenarios. Give this task the time and serious attention it deserves. The foundation of your classroom discipline plan and its success throughout the year is the rules of behavior you set today.

CLASSROOM RULES

WORKSHEET

Use this worksheet to plan your general classroom rules. Remember these guidelines when choosing classroom rules:

- Rules must be observable.
- Rules must be in force at all times, in every class.
- Rules must be appropriate for your students and ones you are comfortable enforcing.

Classroom Rule #1:_____

My rationale for choosing this rule:

_____
_____
_____

Classroom Rule #2:_____

My rationale for choosing this rule:

_____
_____
_____

Classroom Rule #3:_____

My rationale for choosing this rule:

_____
_____
_____

Classroom Rule #4:_____

My rationale for choosing this rule:

_____
_____
_____

Creating Your Classroom Discipline Plan: Positive Recognition

Too often we equate discipline with punishment. Rules are in place to be followed, but it is only when they are broken that we react. A classroom discipline plan that incorporates positive recognition actively motivates students to follow the rules. Rather than using fear of punishment to get kids to behave, it uses the pleasure of positive recognition. Consider what a difference in classroom climate such a plan can make!

The Value of Positive Recognition for Early Adolescents

Positive recognition can be the key to the success of your discipline plan. Yet like those teachers who believe middle-level students should be old enough to know how to behave, some teachers view early adolescents as old enough to follow rules without recognition for doing so.

But the truth is, we all like to be acknowledged for appropriate behavior. And given the unique needs of early adolescents, positive recognition can have an impact beyond creating a more positive classroom climate.

Positive recognition can increase students' self-esteem.

As we reviewed in Chapter 1, early adolescents are extremely sensitive to others' opinions and often suffer from low self-esteem. If the majority of your responses to students are negative, it tears down their self-esteem even more. But if you praise students and help them feel good about themselves, they're more motivated to continue following classroom rules, so that they continue to be recognized positively.

Positive recognition helps you build relationships with students.

We also have talked about the importance of building relationships with students and helping to get to know them as individuals. Positive recognition paves the way to developing rapport because students feel good about being in your classroom. On the other hand, overuse of negative consequences creates tension and pulls teacher and students apart.

Positive recognition discourages students from acting up to get attention.

In most classrooms, who gets more attention, the kids who follow the rules or the disruptive ones? Positive recognition changes the balance. By responding positively to appropriate behavior, you quickly teach students that they can get the attention they want, need and deserve by following the rules.

It's just common sense: The more consistently you use positive recognition to influence students, the better students will feel about you and about being in your classroom, the better you'll feel about yourself, and the more motivated your class will be to achieve your social and academic goals.

Positive recognition puts *positive* peer pressure to work in your classroom. You know that early adolescents want to be accepted by their peers. When it becomes cool *not* to act out, students will do much of the "enforcing" on their own. The disapproval of the group will go a long way toward getting all students to adhere to the rules.

Ideas for Individual Recognition

Just as the rules you set should be appropriate for your students, tailor the means of rewarding behavior to the age and interests of your students. Early adolescence can be a particularly difficult age to know how to reward because the standards of what is cool change quickly. Here are ideas for successful motivators to consider.

Praise

This is the easiest and most meaningful way to provide positive recognition in every class, at any time, every day. When you take time to verbally recognize a student's positive behavior, you are saying "I care about you. I notice the good work you are doing and I'm proud of you."

However, be prepared to deliver praise in different ways depending on your students. Some early adolescents are embarrassed by praise or think it's cool to shrug it off. Don't let that attitude fool you. Personal words of support, enthusiasm and caring are exactly what many "tough" kids need and want to hear. Try delivering compliments quietly, one-on-one. Stand next to the student to praise him or her or write the student a private message of praise. When praising verbally, use casual language, such as a simple "keep it up." Remember, when you know your students well, you're better able to determine the kinds of reinforcement that are most meaningful to each.

Positive notes and phone calls home

This is another highly effective motivator that can reap extra benefits in positive relations with parents. When students follow rules and meet your expectations, let family members know through a positive note home or a quick phone call. That doesn't mean communicating with every family every night. Devote just five minutes a night to positive calls. Plan to call two families—that's ten a week. At that rate, you can reach every family during a semester.

A positive call or note home tells parents that you care about their child's success. You know that parent involvement can be particularly difficult at the middle school level. Such positive recognition can enhance your relationship with parents. By getting good news from the teacher, instead of only hearing from the school when there is a problem, many parents are more inclined to cooperate with you and encourage their child's continued positive behavior. And for the student, it's an acknowledgment of your interest in him or her as an individual. (For sample scripts of positive calls, ready-to-use notes home, a reproducible log for keeping track of positive communication with parents, and other strategies for getting parents on your side, see Chapter 6.)

Special privileges and tangible rewards

While praise and positive notes are powerful motivators for most students, there will be a few for whom they're not. For those students, the chance to earn a special privilege, such as extra computer time, or a tangible reward, such as a coupon good toward purchases at the school store, will be the most effective motivator. However, use these sparingly with individuals. Such incentives can become difficult to manage and expensive for you.

Setting Up a Classwide Recognition System

You can also use special privileges as a behavior incentive for the whole class. You'll need to set up a system for recording positive behavior, such as points on the board; choose a reward you are comfortable giving, such as coupons from the school store; and set a time goal for earning the reward, such as one or two weeks. The classwide system will build on positive peer pressure to encourage all students to behave. A classwide approach also is effective for working on a problem behavior the group is having, such as when students frequently are not in their seats on time.

Let's look more closely at how a classwide system works.

Points on the board.

Designate a corner of the chalkboard to serve as the Classwide Reward Scoreboard. On the scoreboard, write the number of points needed to reach the class reward—let's say 50 over a week's time. Then, when you see a student or group of students behaving appropriately, restate the behavior and put a mark on the board. For example: "Hadi, Jerome, Taneisha and Amy have followed directions and are moving quickly and quietly into their cooperative group. That's a point for the class."

At the start of each class, remind students how many points they've earned and how many they have to go to get their reward: "You've earned 35 points. You have 15 more to earn by Friday for each of you to receive a coupon to the school store."

Set a time goal.

Set a reasonable number of points that students can achieve in one or two weeks. If you allow too much time to achieve the goal, students may lose interest and the incentive to behave. Monitor the frequency with which you are awarding points to ensure that you and the students are on track.

Everyone participates.

All students, regardless of whether they have earned negative consequences individually, should participate in the classwide reward.

Rewards: When in doubt, ask students what they consider to be a motivating means of rewarding appropriate behavior. Naturally, the final decision is yours, but students may think of rewards that you wouldn't.

Give some thought now to which positives you want to incorporate into your classroom discipline plan. Use the "Positive Recognition Plan" worksheet on page 47 to identify them. Be sure that praise is at the top of your list. Remember, too, that the skillful use of positive recognition involves deciding how you, as the teacher, can best meet each student's needs and encourage continued positive behavior.

POSITIVE RECOGNITION PLAN

WORKSHEET

Use this worksheet to outline your plan for using positive recognition to reinforce appropriate classroom behavior. Keep in mind these points as you plan:

• Choose forms of recognition you can apply consistently in the classroom.
• Choose forms that are meaningful to your students.
• Choose forms you are comfortable giving.

Use the "notes to myself" lines to remind yourself of special behaviors or times when you can apply this positive in the classroom, such as during direct instruction or cooperative-group activities.

Positive #1: _____
Notes to myself for using this positive in the classroom:
_____
_____
_____

Positive #2: _____
Notes to myself for using this positive in the classroom:
_____
_____
_____

Positive #3: _____
Notes to myself for using this positive in the classroom:
_____
_____
_____

Positive #4: _____
Notes to myself for using this positive in the classroom:
_____
_____
_____

Creating Your Classroom Discipline Plan: Consequences

Students of all ages need to learn that inappropriate behavior has consequences. For early adolescents, who have the tendency to both push the limits of authority and be ultra sensitive to anything that smacks of partiality, having firm and fair consequences that are applied consistently is key to getting their respect for you and your discipline plan.

Being Prepared for Disruptive Behavior

This third part of your behavior plan involves anticipating those times when students choose not to follow your classroom rules. By carefully planning effective consequences and determining in advance how you will respond when students misbehave, you create a course of action to follow. You are better able to stay calm and avoid escalating the situation, and most important, remain in control of your classroom.

Here are guidelines to follow when choosing consequences:

- Consequences must be something that students do not like.

- Consequences must *never* be physically or psychologically harmful. They must never be meant to embarrass or humiliate a student.

- Consequences do not have to be severe to be effective.

Consequences are not punishment, and that's an important distinction. Punishment usually takes the form of criticism, humiliation and even physical pain—and it breeds resentment. Consequences, on the other hand, are actions students know will occur should they choose to break a classroom rule.

Making Consequences a Choice

Your classroom discipline plan is based on the idea that students are responsible for their own behavior. By clearly stating your behavior expectations in the form of rules, you give students a choice: They can choose to follow the rules, and be recognized for that positive behavior. Or they break those rules, setting a system of consequences in motion.

Here's a sample teacher dialogue that explains how you might present "choosing consequences" to students:

"Roberta, our rule is no shouting out in this classroom. If you shout again, you will have chosen to stay after class for one minute. It's your choice." (After a few minutes, Roberta responds to a student's comment with another outburst.) *"Roberta, you shouted again. You have chosen to stay one minute after class."*

By presenting your consequences as a choice—that the student chooses that a consequence will occur—the misbehaving student cannot be seen as the victim of unfair teacher attention. Equally important, students learn that they are in control of what happens to them.

Consistency Is Key

By assuring that an appropriate consequence always follows an infraction of a classroom rule, you show students that there is a relationship between how they choose to behave and the outcome of that behavior. But you must be consistent in administering consequences. Recall that in Chapter 2 we identified the characteristics of an assertive teacher, and consistency was high on the list. Nonassertive teachers, on the other hand, ignore an inappropriate behavior one day and punish it the next. That inconsistency confuses students and destroys the effectiveness of classroom rules. Are they real? What behavior is acceptable and what is not? On the other hand, when you are consistent in enforcing your rules and automatically respond with a consequence from your behavior plan each time students choose to misbehave, there's no question about what behavior you expect and about what students can expect from you.

Choosing Consequences You Can Enforce Consistently

A mistake teachers can make when establishing consequences is to make them too severe, so that they inconvenience themselves. If you make "stay after school" a consequence, are you sure you'll be able to stay after school each time a student misbehaves? Can you really afford to hold a student for 15 minutes after class when you have another class to teach—or when that 15 minutes cuts into your own planning or lunch time?

As you establish consequences, consider whether you will be able to administer the consequence each and every time. Again, consistency is essential. If you have to make an exception because of your own schedule —*"Okay, I have a meeting after school, so just this one time you don't have to stay after school"*—you've diminished the impact of your consequences.

Many teachers of older students find that a highly effective consequence is having students stay just one minute after class. While that might not seem like enough, teachers who use it report it works like a charm. Young adolescents are always eager to be with their friends, and holding a student for one minute means that his or her friends have moved on, while the student is still in your classroom. Just as important, it's a consequence you can impose without hardship to you or your schedule.

Establishing a System of Graduated Consequences

Your classroom plan needs a discipline hierarchy, so that you are prepared to respond on those days when particular students continue to act out. Remember, the point of a discipline hierarchy is planning, so that you know how you will respond to repeated infractions of the rules.

A discipline hierarchy lists consequences in the order in which they will be imposed for disruptive behavior within a day. The hierarchy is progressive, starting with a warning. The consequences then become gradually more substantial for the second, third, fourth and fifth time a student chooses to disrupt.

Note an important phrase—*within a day*. Try not to carry over consequences to the next day, but there may be exceptions. If you only see Ellen for one period a day, but she constantly breaks the same discipline rule—such as not being in her seat when the bell rings—you may want to inform Ellen that starting this week, the consequences for being late to class will accumulate for her. That may be the only way to help Ellen see you mean business. For other students, starting out the period with a strike or two against them decreases their incentive to behave. You'll need to decide which procedure to follow depending on the individual student.

Let's look at a suggested discipline hierarchy for the middle school:

* **First time a student disrupts: Issue a warning**

  "Adam, the direction was to work without talking. That's a warning."

  Be sure your warning is verbal, so that the student knows without question that he or she has broken a classroom rule. A warning gives the student an opportunity to choose more appropriate behavior before a more substantial consequence is issued.

* **Second time a student disrupts: One minute after class**

  The student has chosen to continue misbehaving, so now provide a consequence. Remember to restate the rule the student did not follow and the consequence, so that there is no question why the student will be staying after class: *"Adam, I gave you a warning. The direction was to work without talking. You have continued to talk. That's one minute after class."*

- **Third time a student disrupts: Two minutes after class and complete a behavior log page**

  You are escalating the consequence, making it more unpleasant for the student while still enabling you to implement. Hold the student for two minutes and give him or her a behavior log to complete—during that time, if possible, or to return to you by class time the next day. You'll find a reproducible "Behavior Journal" worksheet on page 48. It asks the student to reflect on the rule broken and why he or she chose to break that rule. The behavior log helps to reinforce the idea that the student is in control of his or her own actions.

  ### BEHAVIOR *Journal*

  You have chosen to break a classroom rule. Please use this page to reflect on your own behavior. Remember, you are in control of what happens to you. You are responsible for your own actions.

  Name _____ Date _____

  THIS IS THE CLASSROOM RULE I CHOSE NOT TO FOLLOW:
  _____
  _____

  THIS IS WHAT HAPPENED:
  _____
  _____
  _____
  _____

  THIS IS WHY MY BEHAVIOR WAS NOT APPROPRIATE:
  _____
  _____
  _____
  _____

  THIS IS WHAT I COULD HAVE DONE INSTEAD:
  _____
  _____
  _____
  _____

- **Fourth time a student disrupts: Call parents**

  Parent contact is a key component of managing student behavior. In Chapter 6 we'll explain more about the importance of informing parents of your discipline plan and working to enlist their support of it. Naturally, you'll need to decide how to handle parent contact over discipline problems based on each situation and the personalities involved.

- **Fifth time a student disrupts: Send to the principal**

  This should be your last consequence. Imposing it too soon diminishes your sense of control over the behavior in your classroom. Be sure to share your discipline plan with your principal and discuss in advance what kind of action the principal will take when you send students to him or her.

- **Severe clause: Immediate removal from the classroom**

  There may be times when you can't follow a discipline hierarchy and a student must be removed immediately from the classroom. For example, a student might be physically fighting or threatening another student. In such a situation, respond calmly and firmly: *"There is no fighting allowed in this classroom. You know the rule. You have chosen to go to the principal's office immediately. We will discuss this later."*

  If a student severely disrupts the classroom, he or she is stopping the education process. You are unable to teach and other students are unable to learn. You must act immediately to regain control of your classroom. And a severe clause sends a message that certain behaviors are totally out of bounds.

Now, use the "Behavior Consequences Worksheet" on page 49 to choose five consequences and arrange them in a hierarchy from 1 to 5, and to establish a severe clause as well. Remember, just as in setting rules and developing forms of positive recognition, your consequences must be appropriate and meaningful for *your* early adolescents. And keep in mind that your consequences must be *enforceable*. Don't make them more unpleasant for yourself than for your students!

Use the reproducible "Behavior Tracking Sheet" on page 50 to log consequences given for a day or week. Have the sheet discreetly nearby—in your plan book or on your desk. When a student misbehaves, write in the student's name and circle the consequence—1, a warning. If the student breaks the rule again in the same day or week (if you have discussed a weekly time period with the student), circle a 2, one minute after class, and so on. The tracking sheet can also be a helpful means of monitoring overall behavior in each class and at different times of the day.

BEHAVIOR CONSEQUENCES

WORKSHEET

Use this worksheet to plan out your discipline hierarchy. We've filled in the first one—a warning. You always want to give students a chance to stop, think, and change their behavior before you implement a second consequence. Keep these points in mind as you choose consequences for your behavior plan:

- Choose consequences that do not involve humiliating, embarrassing or physically injuring students.
- Make sure you can consistently apply the consequences.

Consequence #1: Warning
Notes to myself for applying this consequence:

_____
_____

Consequence #2: _____
Notes to myself for applying this consequence:

_____
_____

Consequence #3: _____
Notes to myself for applying this consequence:

_____
_____

Consequence #4: _____
Notes to myself for applying this consequence:

_____
_____

Consequence #5 _____
Notes to myself for applying this consequence:

_____
_____

BEHAVIOR TRACKING SHEET

For the week of _____ Class _____

Use this worksheet to keep track of each time a student chooses to misbehave. Circle a 1 for warning, 2 for second consequence, on through your discipline hierarchy.

Name	Monday	Tuesday	Wednesday	Thursday	Friday
_____	1 2 3 4 5	1 2 3 4 5	1 2 3 4 5	1 2 3 4 5	1 2 3 4 5
_____	1 2 3 4 5	1 2 3 4 5	1 2 3 4 5	1 2 3 4 5	1 2 3 4 5
_____	1 2 3 4 5	1 2 3 4 5	1 2 3 4 5	1 2 3 4 5	1 2 3 4 5
_____	1 2 3 4 5	1 2 3 4 5	1 2 3 4 5	1 2 3 4 5	1 2 3 4 5
_____	1 2 3 4 5	1 2 3 4 5	1 2 3 4 5	1 2 3 4 5	1 2 3 4 5
_____	1 2 3 4 5	1 2 3 4 5	1 2 3 4 5	1 2 3 4 5	1 2 3 4 5
_____	1 2 3 4 5	1 2 3 4 5	1 2 3 4 5	1 2 3 4 5	1 2 3 4 5
_____	1 2 3 4 5	1 2 3 4 5	1 2 3 4 5	1 2 3 4 5	1 2 3 4 5
_____	1 2 3 4 5	1 2 3 4 5	1 2 3 4 5	1 2 3 4 5	1 2 3 4 5
_____	1 2 3 4 5	1 2 3 4 5	1 2 3 4 5	1 2 3 4 5	1 2 3 4 5
_____	1 2 3 4 5	1 2 3 4 5	1 2 3 4 5	1 2 3 4 5	1 2 3 4 5
_____	1 2 3 4 5	1 2 3 4 5	1 2 3 4 5	1 2 3 4 5	1 2 3 4 5
_____	1 2 3 4 5	1 2 3 4 5	1 2 3 4 5	1 2 3 4 5	1 2 3 4 5
_____	1 2 3 4 5	1 2 3 4 5	1 2 3 4 5	1 2 3 4 5	1 2 3 4 5
_____	1 2 3 4 5	1 2 3 4 5	1 2 3 4 5	1 2 3 4 5	1 2 3 4 5

Keeping Track of Consequences and Documenting Problem Behavior

For your discipline hierarchy to be effective, you need to keep track each time a student chooses to misbehave. Documenting disruptive behavior also strengthens your case—and demonstrates your professionalism—with parents, administrators and counselors when working through students' problems.

Another valuable form of documentation is anecdotal observations. Take a moment after class or at the end of the day to note problem behaviors that have surfaced. Be specific and factual. Don't state your opinion, state what you observed:

José was loud and boisterous today. He jumped up three times to throw away papers, distracting the class each time. He calmed down after I issued a warning from the discipline plan.

On page 51, you'll find a "Behavior Documentation Sheet" for keeping anecdotal notes on a student whose behavior you are watching closely—either because of demonstrated problems or because of a sudden change in behavior that may signal a serious problem, such as drug or alcohol use.

BEHAVIOR DOCUMENTATION SHEET

STUDENT _____ Grade & Class _____

Date _____ Time _____ Place _____
Description of Problem/Incident: _____
_____
Action Taken: _____
_____
Parent Notified: Yes No   Comments: _____
_____
_____

Date _____ Time _____ Place _____
Description of Problem/Incident: _____
_____
Action Taken: _____
_____
Parent Notified: Yes No   Comments: _____
_____
_____

Date _____ Time _____ Place _____
Description of Problem/Incident: _____
_____
Action Taken: _____
_____
Parent Notified: Yes No   Comments: _____
_____
_____

With whatever form of behavior documentation you use, remember to be specific, be factual, be consistent, and date every observation so that you have a chronological record to support your actions and concerns.

Next Step: Teaching Your Plan

Once you have created your discipline plan, you're on your way to creating a more positive classroom environment, where students know what behavior is expected and what they can expect from you when they follow the rules, as well as when they break them. But do students really know? Does posting rules really ensure they understand your discipline plan and know how to act responsibly?

Think about it: Do you expect students to understand a lesson concept simply by reading some passages in the textbook? Of course not—you actively teach content. The same is true of your discipline plan. You need to teach it, as well as other specific behaviors you expect from students. In the next chapter, we'll offer guidance in putting your plan to work in your classroom.

Use this worksheet to plan your general classroom rules. Remember these guidelines when choosing classroom rules:

- Rules must be observable.
- Rules must be in force at all times, in every class.
- Rules must be appropriate for your students and ones you are comfortable enforcing.

Classroom Rule #1: _____

My rationale for choosing this rule:

_____

_____

_____

Classroom Rule #2: _____

My rationale for choosing this rule:

_____

_____

_____

Classroom Rule #3: _____

My rationale for choosing this rule:

_____

_____

_____

Classroom Rule #4: _____

My rationale for choosing this rule:

_____

_____

_____

Use this worksheet to outline your plan for using positive recognition to reinforce appropriate classroom behavior. Keep in mind these points as you plan:

- Choose forms of recognition you can apply consistently in the classroom.
- Choose forms that are meaningful to your students.
- Choose forms you are comfortable giving.

Use the "notes to myself" lines to remind yourself of special behaviors or times when you can apply this positive in the classroom, such as during direct instruction or cooperative-group activities.

Positive #1: _____

Notes to myself for using this positive in the classroom:

_____

_____

_____

Positive #2: _____

Notes to myself for using this positive in the classroom:

_____

_____

_____

Positive #3: _____

Notes to myself for using this positive in the classroom:

_____

_____

_____

Positive #4: _____

Notes to myself for using this positive in the classroom:

_____

_____

_____

BEHAVIOR *Journal*

You have chosen to break a classroom rule. Please use this page to reflect on your own behavior. Remember, you are in control of what happens to you. You are responsible for your own actions.

Name _____ Date _____

THIS IS THE CLASSROOM RULE I CHOSE NOT TO FOLLOW:

_____

_____

THIS IS WHAT HAPPENED:

_____

_____

_____

_____

_____

THIS IS WHY MY BEHAVIOR WAS NOT APPROPRIATE:

_____

_____

_____

_____

_____

_____

THIS IS WHAT I COULD HAVE DONE INSTEAD:

_____

_____

_____

_____

_____

Use this worksheet to plan out your discipline hierarchy. We've filled in the first one—a warning. You always want to give students a chance to stop, think, and change their behavior before you implement a second consequence. Keep these points in mind as you choose consequences for your behavior plan:

- Choose consequences that do not involve humiliating, embarrassing or physically injuring students.

- Make sure you can consistently apply the consequences.

Consequence #1: Warning

Notes to myself for applying this consequence:

_____

_____

Consequence #2:_____

Notes to myself for applying this consequence:

_____

_____

Consequence #3:_____

Notes to myself for applying this consequence:

_____

_____

Consequence #4:_____

Notes to myself for applying this consequence:

_____

_____

Consequence #5:_____

Notes to myself for applying this consequence:

_____

_____

BEHAVIOR TRACKING SHEET

For the week of _____ **Class** _____

Use this worksheet to keep track of each time a student chooses to misbehave. Circle a 1 for warning, 2 for second consequence, on through your discipline hierarchy.

Name	Monday	Tuesday	Wednesday	Thursday	Friday
_____	1 2 3 4 5	1 2 3 4 5	1 2 3 4 5	1 2 3 4 5	1 2 3 4 5
_____	1 2 3 4 5	1 2 3 4 5	1 2 3 4 5	1 2 3 4 5	1 2 3 4 5
_____	1 2 3 4 5	1 2 3 4 5	1 2 3 4 5	1 2 3 4 5	1 2 3 4 5
_____	1 2 3 4 5	1 2 3 4 5	1 2 3 4 5	1 2 3 4 5	1 2 3 4 5
_____	1 2 3 4 5	1 2 3 4 5	1 2 3 4 5	1 2 3 4 5	1 2 3 4 5
_____	1 2 3 4 5	1 2 3 4 5	1 2 3 4 5	1 2 3 4 5	1 2 3 4 5
_____	1 2 3 4 5	1 2 3 4 5	1 2 3 4 5	1 2 3 4 5	1 2 3 4 5
_____	1 2 3 4 5	1 2 3 4 5	1 2 3 4 5	1 2 3 4 5	1 2 3 4 5
_____	1 2 3 4 5	1 2 3 4 5	1 2 3 4 5	1 2 3 4 5	1 2 3 4 5
_____	1 2 3 4 5	1 2 3 4 5	1 2 3 4 5	1 2 3 4 5	1 2 3 4 5
_____	1 2 3 4 5	1 2 3 4 5	1 2 3 4 5	1 2 3 4 5	1 2 3 4 5
_____	1 2 3 4 5	1 2 3 4 5	1 2 3 4 5	1 2 3 4 5	1 2 3 4 5
_____	1 2 3 4 5	1 2 3 4 5	1 2 3 4 5	1 2 3 4 5	1 2 3 4 5
_____	1 2 3 4 5	1 2 3 4 5	1 2 3 4 5	1 2 3 4 5	1 2 3 4 5
_____	1 2 3 4 5	1 2 3 4 5	1 2 3 4 5	1 2 3 4 5	1 2 3 4 5

BEHAVIOR DOCUMENTATION SHEET

STUDENT _____ **Grade & Class** _____

Date _____ **Time** _____ **Place** _____
Description of Problem/Incident: _____
_____
Action Taken: _____
_____
Parent Notified: Yes No   Comments: _____
_____
_____

Date _____ **Time** _____ **Place** _____
Description of Problem/Incident: _____
_____
Action Taken: _____
_____
Parent Notified: Yes No   Comments: _____
_____
_____

Date _____ **Time** _____ **Place** _____
Description of Problem/Incident: _____
_____
Action Taken: _____
_____
Parent Notified: Yes No   Comments: _____
_____
_____

Putting Your Plan to Work in Your Classroom

Linda Koenig
Junior High Teacher
Nanty Glo, Iowa

"I've become a more assertive teacher and am better able to see the promise of the children we teach, children whom we can help to succeed, now and in the future."

One of the most exciting outcomes of successfully implementing a classroom discipline plan is the opportunity for more positive interactions with students. As students learn to behave responsibly, their potential to succeed socially and academically in your classroom expands.

This chapter will help you use your classroom discipline plan to create an environment that promotes teaching and learning success. There is guidance in teaching the plan—an essential step—as well as tips for implementing your system of rewards and consequences. You'll also find help with promoting more responsible behavior by teaching specific directions and problem-solving skills. By giving students the means to control their own behavior, you offer young adolescents the best shot at fulfilling their promise.

Teaching Your Classroom Discipline Plan

You've developed a classroom discipline plan with rules, rewards, and consequences. *You* know the plan. Now communicate it to students. The time you spend actively teaching your plan will ensure that students will never be able to say, "But I didn't understand that rule . . ."

How should you teach your plan? Just as you would teach academic concepts: Explain why students need rules, rewards, and consequences; outline what each part entails; then check for understanding.

Early adolescents are not new to the idea of rules, rewards, and consequences. In fact, depending on the elementary schools your students come from, they may be quite familiar with the idea of a classroom discipline plan. However, students still need to be taught *your plan*. Remember, your rules, rewards, and consequences are tailored to your unique group of students.

Teaching your plan also gives you an opportunity to emphasize your commitment to it. You know that early adolescents are at a stage when they often test rules and limits. Let students know that your rules are *real* and in force at all times. You will consistently reward students for following those rules. As well, breaking those rules will mean consequences—with no exceptions.

To help you prepare to teach your plan, use the ideas and guidelines that follow, as well as the reproducible planner, "Teaching Your Classroom Discipline Plan," on pages 64-65. Jot down notes and explanations you want to share, then use the planner to outline your presentation to students.

5. Explain your discipline hierarchy:

Consequence #1 _____

_____

Consequence #2 _____

Teaching Your Classroom Discipline Plan

LESSON PLANNING WORKSHEET

Use this worksheet to plan your presentation of your classroom discipline plan to students. Jot down notes and key ideas about the plan that you want to be sure to communicate to students.

1. Why we need rules in the classroom.

_____

_____

2. Explain what each rule means:

Rule #1 _____

Rule #2 _____

Rule #3 _____

Rule #4 _____

Check for understanding: _____

3. Explain your plan for positive recognition.

_____

_____

Check for understanding: _____

4. Why a discipline plan needs consequences.

_____

_____

Continued

Teaching Your Rules

Begin by explaining why classroom rules are necessary: You need to be able to teach and students need to be able to learn. For both actions to occur with the least resistance and greatest success, there must be appropriate behavior in the classroom.

Draw on students' experiences in "playing by the rules" in sports to reinforce this concept. Invite them to share rules of football, baseball, soccer or other team sports and explain the reason for each rule. Encourage students who have jobs out of school, such as baby-sitting and paper routes, to share rules they have to follow. Help students recognize that most rules are in place for safety and to get a job done. Explain that your classroom rules are in place to get your jobs of teaching and learning done. Be sure to state clearly: *"I expect you to follow the rules in my classroom."*

Now review each rule in your discipline plan. State clearly what it means, how it applies in the classroom, and why it's necessary. You know that early adolescents are concerned with fairness. Show students that your rules are not arbitrary. They're in place for students' benefit, as well as your own.

For example, if your first rule is "Follow directions," you might say: *"'Follow directions' means that when I give any direction, such as to open your books or move into cooperative groups, I expect you to follow the direction immediately. Why is this rule necessary? Because we have only 45 minutes in each class period. I don't want to have to take away from that time by repeating directions."*

Finally, check for understanding. Encourage students to ask questions about the rules, and clarify points as needed. Post the rules as a reminder for students. Reiterate that your classroom rules are in force *at all times*.

Share Your Plan for Positive Recognition

Here's your opportunity to set a positive tone in your classroom and take important steps toward building relationships with your students.

Ask students what rewards they receive for following rules in sports or other activities. Responses could include winning the game, feeling good about themselves, and being praised for good sportsmanship.

Explain that you also want to recognize students for observing the classroom rules. State clearly that you are more interested in acknowledging appropriate behavior than inappropriate. You want to "catch students being good."

Share with students the ways you'll recognize them when they choose to follow the rules, such as informing family members through positive notes and phone calls home. Tell students that you will give praise when it's deserved—and that you want it to be considered cool to get a pat on the back in your classroom.

If you'll also be giving out special privileges or tangible rewards, such as no-homework nights or coupons to the school store, explain how students—individually or as a group—can earn those.

This can also be a perfect time to invite students to share ideas for different forms of positive recognition they'd like to receive. You'll want to set guidelines to discourage students from suggesting inappropriate or unrealistic rewards or privileges, but eliciting students' ideas helps you find special ways of acknowledging positive behavior and providing meaningful incentives.

Teaching the Consequences

In advance, post your discipline hierarchy where students can refer to it as you review the consequences of choosing not to follow the rules.

Ask students to tell what happens if they violate a rule in basketball, football or another sport. What are the consequences? They may be removed from the game, or the other team may get a chance to score. Invite your student athletes to confirm that if they break a playing rule, a consequence will automatically follow.

Point out that the same is true in your classroom. If students choose to break a rule, a consequence will automatically follow. Remind students that they are in control of their own actions. When they choose not to follow the rules, they choose for consequences to occur.

Now review your discipline hierarchy with students. Explain that it spells out what will happen the first, second, third, fourth and fifth times a student breaks the same classroom rule, or a different rule, during the same day or week. Here's a sample monologue for explaining a hierarchy to students:

"The first time you choose to disrupt, I give you a verbal warning. That's a chance for you to stop, think, and change your behavior.

"The second time you disrupt, you stay after class one minute past the bell.

"The third time you disrupt, you stay two minutes after class and fill out a behavior journal page. You must fill out all parts and return it to me no later than class time the next day. I expect you to show me that you've really thought about your behavior as you answer the questions on the journal page. (Pass around a blank journal page as a reference.)

"The fourth time you disrupt, I call your parent or grandparent, whoever is in charge in your family. There are no exceptions. Four disruptions in one class is completely unacceptable.

"The fifth time you disrupt, you are sent to the principal.

"You'll also see listed a Severe Clause. This means that if you are fighting or threatening someone—in short, if you are doing something that is preventing me from teaching and other students from learning—you go straight to the principal."

Check to be sure all students understand your discipline hierarchy and each consequence. Depending on how you plan to enforce your rules, explain under what circumstances consequences carry over to the next day.

Close on a positive note by expressing to students your confidence that each one of them is capable of making responsible decisions about classroom behavior.

Implementing Your Classroom Discipline Plan

Okay, you've set your rules, rewards and consequences. You've taught the plan. Now how do you put it into action in your classroom every day? Here are tips that will help enhance the effectiveness of your plan.

Developing the Characteristics of an Assertive Teacher

Build on your classroom discipline plan to help you become an assertive teacher. The plan has already helped you acquire key attributes of an assertive teacher: It has spelled out clearly what you consider to be appropriate behavior in your classroom, and it states fair and consistent consequences for students who choose to behave inappropriately. But an assertive teacher also focuses on the positive. To motivate all students to behave, get in the habit of looking first for students who are behaving appropriately, and acknowledge the behavior with praise.

And that takes practice. For most of us, it's more instinctive to focus first on students who are misbehaving. You've also got your mind on teaching a lesson and keeping everyone on track. It's not easy to also remember to positively recognize students for appropriate behavior.

Creating a P. R. (Positive Reminder) Plan

Find ways to remind yourself during the day to acknowledge positive behavior. Here are some ideas.

Post "Catch them being good" reminders for yourself.

Write it in your plan book or across the top of your lecture notes to nudge yourself to watch for and reinforce positive behavior .

Keep note of whom you praise.

At the start of each class, draw a happy face on a Post-It note, then affix it to your lesson plans or on a clipboard—wherever you can get to it easily and discreetly. Each time you acknowledge a student for positive behavior during class, jot down his or her name or initials. Keep track of whom you praise and how often.

Set a "praise goal" for each class.

For example, try to praise five or so students per period, so that in a week's time, you've acknowledged every student you teach. This can be especially helpful when you're first introducing your plan and praising students consistently is new to you and your kids.

Set a weekly goal for positive notes home.

Remember the importance of positive notes or phone calls home in motivating students and creating rapport with parents. Set a goal of two calls or notes a day, 10 a week—to ensure that you contact each student's family during the semester. (You'll find a set of reproducible "Positive News" notes to send home in Chapter 6.)

Remember to be sensitive to those students who won't want to be singled out publicly for praise. Acknowledge appropriate behavior with handwritten notes, a nod or pat on the back in class, or a quick word with the student after class.

A last word on praise: *Always be sure it's genuine.* If praise is given when it's undeserved, it weakens its effectiveness as a behavior incentive and does little to boost a student's self-esteem. Early adolescents know when their behavior is appropriate and when it's not. And they're very sensitive to actions they consider "phony" on the part of adults. To maintain your own credibility and that of your discipline plan, be sure you acknowledge students only when it's deserved.

Implementing Consequences

Naturally, it's unrealistic to think that your only concern in the classroom will be how to give enough positive recognition. Your discipline plan isn't a magic cure for disruptive behavior. Sometimes a student's behavior will be clearly disruptive and will automatically require a consequence.

For most of us, disciplining is a stressful task. Our heart beats faster and we feel tension rising. It's a natural response to a feeling of being challenged.

But remember, one reason why you've developed your discipline plan is to help you prepare for those times when students choose to misbehave. Use these reminders to help you ensure the effectiveness of that plan.

Remain calm.

The surest way to escalate a situation is to get into a shouting match with a student. Keep your voice even and modulated. Your composure will help calm the misbehaving student and the rest of the class.

Area: Redirecting uptive Behavior

consequences are in place as a means of to behavior that impairs your rights as a ach and students' rights to learn, what es when kids are off task, but not How does your plan help you respond reas of classroom management?

ive teacher, you don't ignore such cause unchecked it can lead to more ehavior. But do you automatically r discipline hierarchy?

w hard and fast rules for managing avior. For nondisruptive off-task e the subtle redirecting techniques that students on task. However, if you find irecting a student twice in one class student needs more structure to help her own behavior.

remember this redirecting technique wn childhood. They may recall a father's expression that told them that as aware of—and disapproved of— behavior. Cultivate such a look to use classroom. When a student is doodling ure, or students working in a group are laughing in a way that tells hot on task, establish eye contact with r group. Without saying a word, give a ook that tells the student(s) that the nappropriate. Maintain eye contact dent(s) is back on task.

roximity

chers move purposefully around the d use their physical presence to ents who are off task. For example, you ent has her head down on her desk. o her, without calling attention verbally to her behavior. Remain there, continuing your lesson, until she rejoins the group. If she's ill, you're in a better position to determine that than if you're across the room.

Mention Student's Name

A third technique is to mention the student's name in a casual but deliberate way. For example, Evan is looking out of the window instead of at the board where you're working through a complicated math equation. You complete the problem, then before starting the next one, you say, "I want everyone, including Evan, to come up with the answer to this problem." Hearing his name brings Evan's attention back where it belongs—on math.

In each situation, once the student is back on track, be sure to acknowledge the appropriate behavior with a "thank you," a smile, or a nod of approval.

Your own good judgment is your most valuable tool in assessing student behavior. Get to know your students well enough so that you know what response from you will be most successful in eliciting appropriate behavior.

Teaching Responsible Behavior

We've talked a lot about the importance of communicating to students what behavior you expect in the classroom. Your classroom discipline plan is an important means of sharing with students the big headlines. Now communicate the fine print.

Too often we make assumptions about what students know and understand about behavior. We think that sixth-, seventh- and eighth-graders, who have been in school for seven or more years, should know how to act when we're lecturing or when we ask them to work together in a group. But those students come to us with experiences from a range of teachers. Some teachers engage students in a lot of group work; others lecture a great deal. Some teachers don't mind noise and moving around.

Other teachers won't tolerate it. To ensure that your students understand what behavior *you* expect during normal academic activities, teach specific directions.

How are these "specific directions" different from your classroom rules? Remember, your classroom rules are in force at all times. The behaviors you expect during a discussion or a class lab are specific to that activity. So while you don't want students moving around during a discussion, such movement is necessary to work in a group or complete a lab. Your litmus test for behavior should be *what allows you to teach and students to learn.*

Identifying Routine Activities and Procedures

Think about the activities and procedures in your classroom and jot them down on a list. They may include some or all of the following:

- Lecture
- Class discussion
- Independent work
- Working in cooperative groups
- Entering the classroom
- Exiting the classroom
- Transitions
- Lab work
- Using computers
- Taking quizzes and tests

Some of these activities and procedures will be more important to you than others. Some will be naturally harder for students to engage in appropriately than others. For example, like many middle school teachers, you may be using more and more cooperative-group activities. But working as a team is a challenge for most students. You'll need to devote more time to teaching specific directions for cooperative-group work than for test taking, for example. Prioritize your list and focus first on the teaching methods you rely on most often.

Use the "Teaching Specific Directions" worksheet on page 66 to help you think through and articulate your behavior expectations for each academic routine. Yes, this will take time, but you'll find that it's time well spent. The effort you put into helping students understand your behavior expectations will make for a better managed classroom in the long run.

As with your classroom rules, keep your directions simple. You don't want to overwhelm students—you want to guide them.

Teaching Specific Directions

Teach specific directions just as you taught your discipline plan. Offer a rationale why particular behaviors are necessary in order for you to teach and students to learn, explain what those specific behaviors are, and check for understanding.

Here's an example of specific directions for a directed lesson and how you might present those directions to students:

"When I'm giving a lesson, it's important to have everyone's attention and involvement. Therefore, we're going to learn exactly what behaviors are expected during a whole-class lesson. These are the directions I expect you to follow:

- *Clear your desks of everything but paper or a notebook for taking notes and a writing tool, a pencil or pen. I'll tell you if you need anything else.*

- *Eyes on me or eyes on your paper. Your eyes should not be looking out of the window or looking at your buddy.*

- *Raise your hand and wait to be called upon to ask a question, answer a question, or respond to something another student has said.*

"Any questions? Okay, then let's review again what I expect you to do during a lecture." (Ask volunteers to restate the directions.)

Here's how you might explain specific directions for a cooperative-group activity:

"Working together as a team is an important way for you to pool your ideas and talents to complete a task. You'll need to be able to work as part of a group when you have a job someday, and I want you to get plenty of practice working cooperatively now.

"There are specific directions I expect you to follow when you work in a cooperative group. Those directions are necessary so that each of you contributes to and learns from the group activity.

"When I give you a cooperative-group activity to complete, this is how I expect you to behave:

- *Move quickly and quietly into your group. You may turn your desks, if needed, to work together.*

- *Review the assignment you have been given. Decide how you can break up the task into parts, so that each member has a specific job to do. Assign a role to each member of the group.*

- *Try to work through the assignment as a group. If you are stuck, raise your hand to signal you need my help. Don't ask other groups for help.*

- *Talk only about the assignment.*

- *Listen carefully to each other. Only one person speaks at a time.*

- *Make sure all group members get a turn to share their ideas and opinions.*

"Any questions? Okay, let's review again what I expect you to do when working in cooperative groups."

Plan to introduce and review specific directions for each different classroom routine you have identified. Review these directions as often as necessary until students demonstrate that they know what behaviors you expect during each different class activity. You'll be amazed at the difference that being specific about how you expect students to behave can make in helping them to behave responsibly.

Teaching Problem-Solving Skills

You can teach your plan; you can teach the behaviors you expect from students when engaged in normal classroom activities. But you cannot anticipate every behavior decision students will need to make. To help students learn to behave responsibly, offer them broader skills to draw on— problem-solving skills.

Granted, that suggestion probably has a familiar ring. Educators at all levels today are encouraged to teach students problem-solving skills. Often the reason cited is to prepare students for the jobs of the future. But problem-solving skills are critical for preparing students for living their lives today. For example, studies of violent young people show that these adolescents have weaker problem-solving skills than less violent peers. When confronted with a problem, kids who choose aggressive behavior may do so because they can't *think* of other alternatives to solve the problem.

Give your students the means to think through appropriate solutions to problems. Teach the steps in problem solving. Problem solve as a group in class. Demonstrate for students how you think through a problem. Make problem-solving skills a goal of advisory activities. The surest way to enhance your own classroom management skills is to help your students learn appropriate ways to respond to the trials and frustrations that are an inevitable part of school life.

Steps in Problem Solving

Share these steps with students. You'll also find them on a handy "Got a Problem?" miniposter on page 67. Hang the poster in the classroom, and give a copy to each student, to tuck in a notebook or keep at home as a helpful reminder.

1. Define the problem.

2. Brainstorm as many solutions as you can.

3. Choose the best idea to try first.

4. Evaluate the results. Did it solve the problem?

   - If so, congratulations!

   - If not, try another solution.

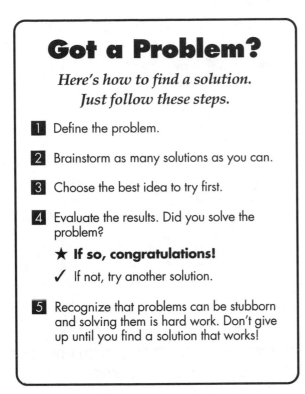

Got a Problem?

Here's how to find a solution.
Just follow these steps.

1 Define the problem.

2 Brainstorm as many solutions as you can.

3 Choose the best idea to try first.

4 Evaluate the results. Did you solve the problem?

★ **If so, congratulations!**

✓ If not, try another solution.

5 Recognize that problems can be stubborn and solving them is hard work. Don't give up until you find a solution that works!

---

5. Recognize that problems can be stubborn and solving them is hard work. Don't give up until you find a solution that works.

Guiding your students to be better problem solvers will do double duty in your classroom, whatever you teach. Students will learn to think more clearly—about content and their own behavior.

Your Next Step: Garnering Parent Support for Your Discipline Plan

There's one more critical step involved in putting your discipline plan to work in your classroom, and that's informing parents of it and encouraging their support of your behavior policies at home. Granted, parent relations at the middle school are particularly complex, and one of the biggest challenges is often getting parents to show consistent involvement in their young adolescents' school life. In the next chapter, we'll explore successful strategies for getting parents on your side.

LESSON PLANNING WORKSHEET

Use this worksheet to plan your presentation of your classroom discipline plan to students. Jot down notes and key ideas about the plan that you want to be sure to communicate to students.

1. Why we need rules in the classroom.

_____

_____

_____

2. Explain what each rule means:

Rule #1 _____

_____

Rule #2 _____

_____

Rule #3 _____

_____

Rule #4 _____

_____

Check for understanding: _____

3. Explain your plan for positive recognition.

_____

_____

_____

Check for understanding: _____

4. Why a discipline plan needs consequences.

_____

_____

_____

Continued

5. Explain your discipline hierarchy:

Consequence #1 _____

_____

Consequence #2 _____

_____

Consequence #3 _____

_____

Consequence #4 _____

_____

Consequence #5 _____

_____

Severe Clause: _____

_____

Check for understanding: _____

Use this worksheet to think through the behaviors you expect from students when engaged in a particular type of classroom activity or procedure, such as entering the classroom, participating in a discussion, working in a cooperative group, listening to a lesson. Draw on these notes when teaching the specific directions to students.

Activity: _____

Specific Directions I Will Teach for this Activity:

_____
_____
_____
_____
_____

Key Points I Will Cover in Teaching Activity to Students:

Rationale:

_____
_____
_____
_____

Specific Behaviors Expected:

_____
_____
_____
_____
_____
_____
_____
_____

Ask questions and check for understanding.

Got a Problem?

Here's how to find a solution.
Just follow these steps.

1 Define the problem.

2 Brainstorm as many solutions as you can.

3 Choose the best idea to try first.

4 Evaluate the results. Did you solve the problem?

★ **If so, congratulations!**

✓ If not, try another solution.

5 Recognize that problems can be stubborn and solving them is hard work. Don't give up until you find a solution that works!

Getting Parents on Your Side

Paul Held
Middle School Teacher
Westport, Connecticut

"Having parent support has truly improved my classroom, and my students are the richer for it."

It's amazing what a difference a successful discipline plan can make in your classroom. Because you have spelled out the behavior you expect from students—both general rules, as well as specific directions for the normal routines of learning—you can devote more time to *teaching*. You can approach daily life in the classroom more calmly and with greater confidence because you have a plan for how you will respond each time students choose to disrupt. And because your discipline plan also helps you to focus on the positive—on students whose behavior is appropriate—your expectation of success is higher. A classroom discipline plan opens doors to greater success and satisfaction as a teacher.

Overcoming negative beliefs is a big part of such a transformation. Positive, assertive teachers believe in their ability to communicate with students and to draw the best from them—in behavior and learning. And positive, assertive teachers also believe in their ability to build relationships with parents and to garner support at home for their discipline plan at school.

This chapter will guide you in using the attributes of an assertive teacher to reach out to parents and build alliances with them. By planting the seeds of a positive relationship from the start, you'll find that even hard-to-reach middle school parents are willing to work with you and welcome your insights into the often contradictory behavior of their early adolescents.

Throughout the chapter, *parent* is meant to represent the person or persons who fill the parenting role in a student's life. Whether it's a grandmother, aunt or an adult sibling, that person plays a key role in the student's life. Reach out to that adult. You, and the student, have everything to gain.

Informing Parents of Your Discipline Plan

Once you've developed your classroom discipline plan and taught it to students, share it with parents or other adult family members. They're part of the plan. Positive notes and phone calls home are ways you will recognize students for appropriate behavior. On those occasions when students choose to disrupt repeatedly, a call to parents may be part of your discipline hierarchy. You need to inform parents in advance of these plans, so that they understand the significance of both positive and problem calls or notes from you.

Sharing the Plan

Prepare a letter that outlines your plan—rules, rewards, and consequences. Explain your rationale for having a classroom discipline plan. Help parents recognize that your plan protects students' rights to be treated fairly and consistently by you. It also protects your rights as a teacher to teach and the rights of all of the students in the class to have an environment suitable for learning.

If your team has adopted a teamwide discipline plan, send the letter from the team. Let parents know that your team is united in your behavior expectations for all students and that the rules and consequences of one teacher are the same for all.

On the next page is a sample letter that introduces parents to your discipline plan. (You'll also find it as a ready-to-reproduce letter on page 83.) Naturally, adapt it to fit your own plan and personality.

Dear Parent,

I am delighted that _____ is in my _____ class this year. Your child will participate in and enjoy many exciting and rewarding experiences this school year.

Because your child's success in school depends in large part on working in an environment that is safe and caring, I have developed a classroom discipline plan that includes rules that will guide every student in making responsible choices about his or her behavior. Here is an outline of the plan.

RULES:
1._____
2._____
3._____
4._____

POSITIVE RECOGNITION to encourage students to follow these rules:
_____
_____

CONSEQUENCES: If a student chooses to break a rule, the following steps will be taken, in the order they appear.

First time a student breaks a rule:
Second time: _____
Third time: _____
Fourth time: _____
Fifth time: _____
Severe Disruption: _____

Your child has been thoroughly informed of the plan. Please review it together at home. Then tear off the form below, sign it, and have your child return it to me. I also welcome your comments or questions about the plan.

My goal is to work with you to ensure your child's success this year. The middle school years are a pivotal time for young adolescents. They need our guidance to grow up to be healthy, happy adults. Together, we can help build a bright future for your child!

Sincerely,

- -

I have read and understand the classroom discipline plan.

(Parent or Guardian)_____

Comments: _____
_____

Dear Parent,

I am delighted that (student's name) is in my (subject area) class this year. Your child will participate in and enjoy many exciting and rewarding experiences this school year.

Because your child's success in school depends in large part on working in an environment that is safe and caring, I have developed a classroom discipline plan that includes rules that will guide every student in making responsible choices about his or her behavior. Here is an outline of the plan.

Rules:

1. Follow directions.

2. Be in your seat when the bell rings.

3. No fighting, swearing, or teasing.

4. Keep hands, feet, and objects to yourself.

Positive Recognition:

To encourage students to follow these rules, I will recognize appropriate behavior with praise, and occasionally, with positive notes and phone calls to you.

Consequences:

If a student chooses to break a rule, the following steps will be taken, in the order they appear:

- *First time a student breaks a rule: Verbal warning*

- *Second time: Stay 1 minute after class*

- *Third time: Stay 2 minutes after class and fill out a behavior journal*

- *Fourth time: Call parent*

- *Fifth time: Send to principal*

- *Severe Disruption: Send to principal immediately*

Your child has been thoroughly informed of the plan. Please review it together at home. Then tear off the form below, sign it, and have your child return it to me. I also welcome your comments or questions about the plan.

My goal is to work with you to ensure your child's success this year. The middle school years are a pivotal time for young adolescents. They need our guidance to grow up to be healthy, happy adults. Together, we can help build a bright future for your child!

Getting Parent Feedback on the Plan

Include a means of determining that every parent receives the letter and is informed of the plan. For instance, as noted in the sample letter, include a tear-off form that provides a place for the parent's signature as well as blank lines where parents can comment or ask questions about the plan.

Follow up on these comments and questions with notes or, preferably, personal phone calls. It's an ideal opportunity to establish open communication lines with parents and to express your appreciation of their interest and support.

Make extra copies of the letter, so that you are ready to send one home with each new student who enters your class throughout the year. Parent conferences and Back-to-School Nights are also good times to discuss the plan with family members.

Building Parent Support from the Start

Imagine you're two months into the school year and you've never spoken directly with your principal. You've received some form letters, but nothing addressed specifically to you. Now the first contact you have—by phone or in writing—is about a problem. How does that make you feel?

When it comes to parent relations, one of the biggest traps we as educators fall into is to make our first contact with parents a discussion about a problem. Parents tend to be defensive and often we're left with two problems—a disruptive student and an uncooperative parent.

Build a foundation for parent-teacher relations. Start the year *literally* on a positive note. Make your first communication with parents a positive one expressing your pleasure at having their children in your class for the first time or again this year. In fact, this note will be even more meaningful if parent and child receive it in the weeks before school begins. For your convenience, you'll find a sheet of welcome notes, ready to reproduce, on page 84.

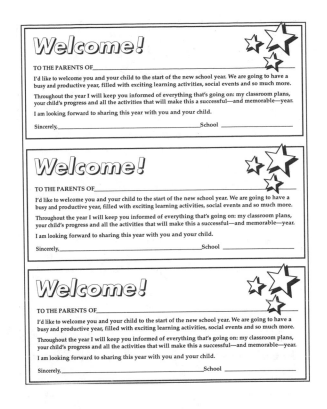

The Time Factor

Perhaps about now you're thinking, "That's great, but I don't have time to write 130 parents."

Parent contact is a bigger challenge for middle-level teachers. Unlike primary or elementary teachers, who may have 25 to 30 students in a class, you may have five or six classes a day with that many students. Reaching every parent is a time-consuming prospect.

But it's not impossible. And the time you spend now in building rapport with parents will pay off. Consider the time, energy and anxiety you expend on difficult and disruptive students. Often the parents of these students are the ones whose support you need in the greatest way. Yet these are also the parents who, over the years, have been on the receiving end of plenty of bad news from school. These are the parents who are most likely to be defensive and angry when you call home with a problem. Conversely, they're also the parents who may be most surprised—and pleased—to receive a positive message from you at the start of the year.

As you weigh the time involved in positive parent contact, consider these benefits:

You're sending a message that middle school isn't impersonal.

In many situations, the middle school is much larger and farther away than the elementary school a student has come from. Because the school is bigger, and perhaps no longer a "neighborhood" school, parents may assume that the way of doing things there—including parent-teacher relations—is more impersonal. By sending home a personal note of welcome and inviting parents to join you in making this school year a successful one for their children, you communicate that parent involvement is every bit as important in middle school as it was during the elementary years.

You offer parents an ally in working with (and coping with) their early adolescents.

If teaching early adolescents is tough, parenting them is even tougher! You know that many parents struggle to cope with the ups and downs of early adolescence. They may view their children's efforts to define their own selves, to form new relations with peers, and to move beyond the bonds and bounds of family with confusion, exasperation, sadness, anger—or all of the above. Parents can benefit greatly from your understanding of the developmental process their children are going through and your calm assurance that, in most cases, their kids' actions and moods are perfectly normal. They also can benefit from your guidance—and example through your discipline plan—of what early adolescents still need, which is firm and fair behavior boundaries.

You, too, can benefit from such alliances. Most parents are the experts on their children. They have the greatest insights on and influence over their child. They can bolster your positives and back up your consequences in ways that will increase the effectiveness of your discipline plan exponentially.

You are in a better position to influence parents to influence their kids to stay in school.

You know that many parents have very unpleasant memories of school. Parents who dropped out or just made it out of high school may have children who do the same. Yet, it's not too late in middle school to set future dropouts on a different, more promising course. Reaching out to all parents, demonstrating your commitment to their child's future success, and encouraging their support of the same, has much greater potential to turn parent and student attitudes around.

Tips for Positive Home Communication

Here are ideas for managing positive home-school communication with greater ease and success.

If you are disciplining as a team, make it a team effort to contact families.

You'll make short work of contacting the parent of every student on your team if you share the job of sending out notes. Agree on the text for one simple welcome greeting, then have every team member sign his or her name and subject area before duplicating the note on school stationary. Or your team might design special team stationary on which the notes can go, as well as other correspondence throughout the year. Aside from the obvious benefit of splitting four or five ways the job of mailing notes, a greeting from the team tells parents that you'll be acting in collaboration. If parent-team conferences will be a new experience for parents, this early show of unity will help them get used to the notion of interacting with their child's teachers as a group.

Set up a schedule for sending out a few before-school welcoming notes every day.

If you don't have the support of a team for this task, trying to send out 130 notes in the week before school starts will naturally overwhelm you. Plan to begin the month before opening day. Break up the task so you can do it comfortably—such as sending out six or seven notes a day.

Keep your notes or phone calls simple and friendly.

You don't have to write or say a lot to have an impact on parent and student alike. Here's a sample welcoming note before school begins:

August 10

Dear Mr. and Mrs. Owen:

I am so pleased that Keisha will be in my seventh-grade history class. We're planning an exciting year of projects and study that I'm confident Keisha will learn from and enjoy. I look forward to working with you to help make seventh grade a successful and special year for Keisha!

Here's what a positive note home might say once school begins:

September 28

Dear Ms. Daniel:

It's a pleasure to let you know what a terrific job Jeff is doing in my class. Every day he comes to class on time and settles down to work right away. I think you'll see better grades this year because of his responsible behavior. You should be very proud of the effort he's making.

Here's what a positive phone call to a parent might sound like:

"Hello, Dr. Jabar. This is Rebecca Peterson, Ahmed's math teacher. I wanted you to know that Ahmed is setting a wonderful example for the other students in my math class. He follows my directions as soon as I give them. His peers know and appreciate that he has earned them quite a few points toward special privileges in our classwide reward system.

"I just wanted you to know how pleased I am that Ahmed has made such a great start to eighth grade. I'm confident he's going to have a very good year. Please tell him that I called."

Set up a loose timetable for sending communication home, particularly at the beginning of the year. For example, following this outline, you'll have four chances for positive communication with parents in the first months of school:

- Welcome note.

- Discipline plan.

- Positive behavior note.

- Invitation to Open House or a special program at school.

Use the "Welcome Notes" and "Positive News" forms, with lines for personalizing each message, on pages 84 and 85. Copy these, so that you're always ready when a student's positive behavior in the classroom deserves a pat on the back at home.

Monitor your positive communication with parents.

To help you keep track of your progress, use the "Tracking Positive Communication" sheet on page 86. Copy it as many times as needed to have a space for each student. Then each time you send a "good news" note or make a positive call, mark it on the sheet. You can see at a glance which students have yet to get this form of positive recognition from you.

TRACKING POSITIVE COMMUNICATION

Class/Grade_____

Use this page to keep track of your use of notes, phone calls, and other means of positive communication between school and home. Circle an N for note, PC for phone call, and O for other, such as a positive conversation with a parent at a school event or in the community. Make your goal positive communication with each student's family at least once a semester.

Name	Month of	Month of	Month of	Month of	Month of
_____	N PC O	N PC O	N PC O	N PC O	N PC O
_____	N PC O	N PC O	N PC O	N PC O	N PC O
_____	N PC O	N PC O	N PC O	N PC O	N PC O
_____	N PC O	N PC O	N PC O	N PC O	N PC O
_____	N PC O	N PC O	N PC O	N PC O	N PC O
_____	N PC O	N PC O	N PC O	N PC O	N PC O
_____	N PC O	N PC O	N PC O	N PC O	N PC O
_____	N PC O	N PC O	N PC O	N PC O	N PC O
_____	N PC O	N PC O	N PC O	N PC O	N PC O
_____	N PC O	N PC O	N PC O	N PC O	N PC O
_____	N PC O	N PC O	N PC O	N PC O	N PC O
_____	N PC O	N PC O	N PC O	N PC O	N PC O
_____	N PC O	N PC O	N PC O	N PC O	N PC O
_____	N PC O	N PC O	N PC O	N PC O	N PC O

Remember the rule of thumb for positive communication home: two positive calls or notes a day for 10 a week. Within the first three months of school, nearly every parent will have heard positive news about his or her child's performance at school.

Contacting Parents When Problems Arise

The first time you call a parent about a problem—and the parent supports *you*—you'll fully realize the value of sharing good news with parents before you have reason to share the bad.

Your notes of welcome and praise signal to parents that you have their children's best interests at heart. Naturally, there will always be some parents who defend their kids no matter what; but in many more cases, your positive communication plan will lay a foundation for more cooperative relations with parents when problems arise. These strategies, too, will help support you in these situations.

Keep Communication Lines Open

In Chapter 4 we reviewed the importance of documenting behavior problems. However, the need to document problems doesn't mean you wait until you have a stack of cards detailing disruptive behaviors before you notify parents. Contact them at the first sign of a problem. Whether it's an academic or behavioral concern, don't let it fester until it is out of hand. If you want parent support, you've got to let them know what's happening with their child at school.

Phone calls are the best means of working through a problem. Yes, they take more time than writing a note, and it's never easy to make a call that could be potentially explosive. But if you have used a positive approach to set the stage for good relations, you'll defuse some of the defensiveness a parent may feel. And a personal phone call allows the give-and-take of conversation. It enables you to make sure the parent understands the situation fully and lets you answer questions and clarify misunderstandings on the spot.

Making a Problem Call

Plan what you want to say before you make the call. You'll be more articulate and better prepared when you've taken the time to think about how you want to present the problem to the parent. Use the "Planning a Problem Phone Call Worksheet: Initial Call" on page 87 to help you plan out problem phone calls.

Planning a Problem Phone Call Worksheet

For the Initial Call About a Problem

Date of call_____
Student:_____ Grade/Class:_____
Parent or Guardian_____
Home phone _____ Work phone _____

Jot down points you want to cover in each of these areas during the call.

Statement of concern:_____

Describe the specific problem or behavior:_____
_____

Describe steps you've taken so far:_____

Get parent input on the problem:_____

Record parent's comments:_____

Present ideas for solutions:
 • What you'll do at school:_____

 • What you'd like parent to do at home:_____

Reassure parent problem can be solved:_____
_____

Describe the follow-up contact parent can expect:_____
_____

Notes:_____
_____
_____

Here are some guidelines to follow when making problem calls:

Start with a statement of concern.

"Ms. Jackson, I'm calling because I'm concerned about David's behavior in my class."

Describe the specific behavior that necessitated the call.

"David is frequently off task—staring out the window, doodling, putting his head on his desk. He's not paying attention and he hasn't been doing his homework. This week he has not turned in a single assignment on time. But when I ask him why he's late with his homework, he doesn't have an answer."

Describe the steps you have taken to solve the problem.

"At first I tried talking to him, to be sure he understood the work and to emphasize that I wanted his attention during class. When that didn't turn around his behavior, I used the consequences in my discipline plan. Yesterday, after a warning, I kept him one minute after class. I have spoken with him on three occasions about the need to complete his work, including homework assignments."

Get parental input.

"Is there anything you can tell me that might help explain David's behavior and help us to get him back on track, so that he is paying attention in class and completing his homework on time?"

Present your solution to the problem.

"Here's what I'll do at school: I'll continue to praise David and give him other kinds of positive reinforcement when he pays attention and contributes during class. When I give a homework assignment, I'll make sure David understands thoroughly what needs to be done, and I'll also look for ways to reward him positively when he turns his homework in on time. When his behavior is not appropriate in class, then David will have chosen for the consequences in our class discipline plan to be imposed. And if he continues not to do his homework, his grade will suffer.

"I'd like you to let David know I called and that I'm concerned about his work and behavior. Please tell him that you're concerned, too. I'd like the two of you to talk about his homework problems. Perhaps he needs a quieter place at home where he can study. I think the most important thing for David to know is that we are working together to help him do better in school."

Express confidence in your ability to solve this problem.

"Ms. Jackson, I've found that seventh grade is a difficult year for many students. I know that David did well in sixth grade and is certainly capable of doing good work this year. I know that together we can help David improve his behavior."

Let the parent know you'll follow up.

"I'll call you again in a week to let you know how things are going in school. Please feel free to call me at school in the meantime."

Key points about this call:

- The teacher comes across as calm and concerned.

- The teacher doesn't blame the parent for the child's behavior or in any way put the parent on the defensive.

- The teacher states clearly what the problem is and what he or she has done thus far to solve it.

- The teacher states what he or she will do next and gives the parent some ideas of what she can do at home to help.

- The teacher tells the parent that there will be further contact on this issue and encourages open communication lines by inviting the parent to initiate calls as well.

- By keeping the tone of the call one of concern and not accusation, the teacher opens the way to obtain vital information about changes in family life that would help explain this student's behavior.

If, by the time designated for the next call, the student's behavior has improved, the teacher relates the positive changes to the parent and encourages her to continue supporting the student's behavior at home with praise and special privileges. If, however, the problem has not improved, the teacher follows the same steps in the follow-up call. Use the "Planning a Problem Phone Call Worksheet: Follow-Up Call" on page 88 to plan for such calls when necessary.

Planning a Problem Phone Call *Worksheet*

*For a **Follow-up Call** About a Problem*

Date of call:_____

Student:_____ Grade/Class:_____

Parent or Guardian:_____

Home phone:_____ Work phone: _____

Jot down points you want to cover in each of these areas during the call.

Statement of concern about student's continuing problem: _____

Describe the specific problem or behavior:_____

Review what you agreed on in the previous call as ways to help solve the problem:_____

_____

Get parent input on the continuing problem:_____

Record parent's comments: _____

Present new ideas for solutions:
- What you'll do at school:_____

- What you'd like parent to do at home:_____

Reassure parent, then describe next steps if problem persists:_____

_____

Notes:_____

_____

_____

Next Step: Conducting a Problem-Solving Conference

When phone calls don't correct a problem, you need to meet with the parent or guardian.

Decide first who will be involved in the conference. If you are disciplining as a team, or if the student is having the same problems in every class, it makes sense to meet with the parent as a group. You'll have more impact on the student if all of his or her teachers can work together with the parent to find ways to support the student and change the problem behavior. Keep these considerations in mind when conducting a problem-solving conference as a team:

Inform the parent that he or she will meet with the team.

Make sure the parent knows in advance who will be at the meeting. Surprising a parent with the news that "a few of Amy's other teachers decided to join us" is sure to overwhelm or anger the parent, and at the least will start the meeting on the wrong foot.

Explain that the team's goal is consistent action in support of the student.

You'll also help to dispel any feeling that the team is "ganging up" on the parent by explaining your rationale for meeting as a team. Emphasize that your goal is to establish a consistent approach that all members of the team and the parent agree on. Inviting all parties concerned to talk face to face is the most productive way to achieve that end.

Bring in a moderator to ensure the parent has an equal voice.

Even in the most congenial setting, a parent is likely to feel outnumbered. Invite a nonteam member to moderate the meeting and ensure the parent's views are heard.

Decide whether the student should attend, too.

One of the best reasons for having the student present is to demonstrate the solidarity of teachers and parent in wanting to help. This can have a strong impact on early adolescents, who while struggling to declare their independence, also still want and need the support of key adults in their lives. Involving the student in the problem-solving process also demonstrates your belief that he or she is capable of behaving responsibly. Finally, the student may be needed to provide information or answer questions about his or her behavior.

However, here again is why it's so important to know your students well. If you believe the student will be disruptive or that the parent will be too uncomfortable, then it's better not to include the student. Your goal is a productive meeting. Don't put obstacles in the way of meeting your goal.

Planning the Conference Specifics

Just as with a problem phone call home, you need to think through this conference in advance. Use the "Planning a Problem-Solving Conference" worksheet on page 89 to organize your comments and the direction of the meeting.

If you'll be meeting with the parent as a team, have each member of the team fill out the sheet, then sit down together before the conference to review your individual responses. *Make sure you agree on the problem at hand and on the best approach to solving it.* Agree as a group on what you'll do at school to support the student and what you would like the parent to do at home. Choose one team member to be the chief spokesperson for the group. If you wait until the actual conference to sort out your differences, you'll confuse the parent and dampen the sense of team solidarity.

Planning a Problem-Solving Conference

Student: _____ Grade/Class: _____

Parent or Guardian _____

Names of teachers/others who will attend: _____
_____

Date of conference: _____

Jot down points you want to cover in each of these areas during the conference.

Statement of concern about student's continuing problem: _____

Describe the specific problem and present documentation: _____
_____

Review what has already been done to solve the problem: _____

Get parent input on the problem: _____

Get student input on the problem (if present) : _____
_____

Present new ideas for solutions:

• What you'll do at school: _____

• What you'd like parent to do at home: _____
_____

Reassure parent, then describe next steps if problem persists: _____
_____

Notes: _____
_____
_____

Gather your documentation records to bring to the conference. Some parents will only be moved to act by such proof of severe or chronic misbehavior. Be sure your records are in chronological order, so that you can present a coherent picture of the problem behavior and your ongoing efforts to correct it.

Encourage a Supportive Atmosphere

Throughout the meeting, let your rule of thumb be, "How would I feel if I were the parent in this situation?" Be firm in your resolve to solve the problem and professional in your manner, but at the same time, demonstrate your concern for the parent's feelings. Thank the parent for making the time to meet with you. State your reason for holding this meeting, and make it clear that you're not looking to assign blame. Then, as you work through your conference plan, show respect for the parent's views and be willing to listen to criticisms of school policies or of your classroom policies that may be justified.

For example, let's say that David is still not doing homework assignments. In the course of the conference, David's mother raises the possibility that David is overwhelmed by the amount of homework he's getting from all of his teachers. She wonders if the team members are aware of how much homework they each give. She may have a valid point. Rather than dismissing the idea, assure her that the team will review their homework assignments together and analyze whether the collective amount could be overwhelming for some students. For many parents, that's all they're asking—that you consider their point of view. Doing so is the best way of getting a parent to respect yours.

Ensuring a Parent's Continuing Support

You've had a good meeting and come to clear agreement on how you will support the student at home and school. You're ready to do your part at school. But what about the parent? You know that parents mean well, but the resolve of a meeting can slip away in the face of everyday demands. How can you provide constant support and reminders, without seeming to badger the parent?

A home-school contract is one solution. It's a written agreement between teacher, parent, and student. The student agrees to a particular behavior—for example, to come to class on time every day, with all books and necessary materials, and with homework completed. Both teacher and parent agree to respond to the student's behavior with specific positives when the student adheres to the terms of the agreement, and with specific consequences when he or she does not.

When should a home-school contract be used? Here are guidelines. Use it when:

- the student will benefit from a structured, individualized system of positives and consequences.

- other solutions to the problem have not worked.

- the student would benefit from more positive reinforcement from the parent.

- the parent has specifically asked for your help in solving a problem.

Presenting the Contract

Introduce the contract during the problem-solving conference. In a team conference, draw up one contract for team, parent, and student.

Explain the purpose of the contract. If the student is present, spend some time talking about what a *contract* is and how it's used in business transactions of all kinds. Emphasize that signing a contract to buy a home or agree to do a job is serious business in the adult world. Your home-school contract should be viewed just as seriously. With the parent, stress consistency in using praise and other positives to reward appropriate behavior and in following through with consequences when the student chooses not to adhere to the terms of the contract.

Using the "Home-School Contract" sheet on page 90, fill in each part of the contract. These steps will guide you:

Home–School Contract

Student:_____ Grade/Class:_____

Behavior student agrees to:_____
_____

Each day_____**follows the terms of the contract, the
following positive reinforcement will be given:**
• by the undersigned teacher or team
_____
_____
_____

• by the parent
_____
_____
_____

Each day_____**does not follow the terms of the contract,
the following consequences will be given:**
• by the undersigned teacher or team
_____
_____

• by the parent
_____
_____

Contract is in effect from _____ **to**_____
Student's signature: _____
Parent's signature: _____
Teacher: _____ Teacher: _____
Teacher: _____ Teacher: _____

Determine the desired behavior from the student.

Working through the problem-solving sheet helped you identify the problem. Now state on the contract how you want the student to behave.

Detail the positive praise, privileges, and rewards you'll give the student for following the terms of the contract.

These might include a homework pass, positive notes home or a special reward, such as a free ticket to a school or community event.

Help the parent identify positives to use at home.

Parent support and praise are vital in this enterprise. Brainstorm ideas for privileges the child will find motivating and the parent can *consistently* employ. Remind the parent that the cheapest, easiest, and most meaningful way of positively reinforcing appropriate behavior is sincere words of praise.

Explain the negative consequences you'll employ when the student chooses not to comply.

Whatever you decide, be it having the student stay one minute after class or calling the parent at home, carry it out consistently.

Help the parent choose consequences to use at home.

Again, having the parent back up your consequences at home is critical. Brainstorm appropriate consequences the parent feels able to impose consistently, such as no television or phone privileges, grounding the child for a specific period of time, and so on.

Decide on the duration of the contract.

Choose a length of time that you and the parent can live up to. For a young adolescent, two to four weeks is reasonable. Remember, you want the student to succeed. Don't set unreachable goals.

Have all parties sign it.

When presenting the contract to the student, emphasize that it's not a punishment. It's an opportunity to help the student make a positive change in behavior.

Maintain daily contact with the parent.

Each day the contract is in effect, send home a note updating the parent on the student's behavior. Include in your note the date, how the student acted in class, what action you took (positive or negative consequence), and what the parent should do at home. For your convenience, you'll find a follow-up "Home-School Contract Communication Form" on page 91.

When Students Persist in Being Disruptive...

For many students, a home-school contract will be a viable solution to behavior problems. But for some difficult young adolescents, you'll need many more approaches and all the parent and administrative support you can muster to maintain your composure and the control of your classroom. In the next chapter, you'll find strategies for succeeding with difficult students.

Home-School Contract
COMMUNICATION FORM

Student's Name _____ Date: _____

Dear _____

☐ Today your child behaved according to the terms of the contract. I have given the positive reinforcement that we agreed upon. Please follow through at home with your positive reinforcement, also.

☐ Today your child did not behave according to the terms of the contract. I have given the negative consequences that we agreed upon. Please follow through at home with your negative consequences, also.

Please contact me if you have any questions or if you would like to talk about the contract.

Sincerely, _____

Additional comments: _____
_____

Home-School Contract
COMMUNICATION FORM

Student's Name _____ Date: _____

Dear _____

☐ Today your child behaved according to the terms of the contract. I have given the positive reinforcement that we agreed upon. Please follow through at home with your positive reinforcement, also.

☐ Today your child did not behave according to the terms of the contract. I have given the negative consequences that we agreed upon. Please follow through at home with your negative consequences, also.

Please contact me if you have any questions or if you would like to talk about the contract.

Sincerely, _____

Additional comments: _____
_____

Dear Parent,

I am delighted that _____ is in my _____ class this year. Your child will participate in and enjoy many exciting and rewarding experiences this school year.

Because your child's success in school depends in large part on working in an environment that is safe and caring, I have developed a classroom discipline plan that includes rules that will guide every student in making responsible choices about his or her behavior. Here is an outline of the plan.

RULES:

1. _____

2. _____

3. _____

4. _____

POSITIVE RECOGNITION to encourage students to follow these rules:

_____

_____

CONSEQUENCES: If a student chooses to break a rule, the following steps will be taken, in the order they appear.

First time a student breaks a rule:

Second time: _____

Third time: _____

Fourth time: _____

Fifth time: _____

Severe Disruption: _____

Your child has been thoroughly informed of the plan. Please review it together at home. Then tear off the form below, sign it, and have your child return it to me. I also welcome your comments or questions about the plan.

My goal is to work with you to ensure your child's success this year. The middle school years are a pivotal time for young adolescents. They need our guidance to grow up to be healthy, happy adults. Together, we can help build a bright future for your child!

Sincerely,

- -

I have read and understand the classroom discipline plan.

(Parent or Guardian) _____

Comments: _____

_____

Welcome!

TO THE PARENTS OF _____

I'd like to welcome you and your child to the start of the new school year. We are going to have a busy and productive year, filled with exciting learning activities, social events and so much more.

Throughout the year I will keep you informed of everything that's going on: my classroom plans, your child's progress and all the activities that will make this a successful—and memorable—year.

I am looking forward to sharing this year with you and your child.

Sincerely, _____ School _____

Welcome!

TO THE PARENTS OF _____

I'd like to welcome you and your child to the start of the new school year. We are going to have a busy and productive year, filled with exciting learning activities, social events and so much more.

Throughout the year I will keep you informed of everything that's going on: my classroom plans, your child's progress and all the activities that will make this a successful—and memorable—year.

I am looking forward to sharing this year with you and your child.

Sincerely, _____ School _____

Welcome!

TO THE PARENTS OF _____

I'd like to welcome you and your child to the start of the new school year. We are going to have a busy and productive year, filled with exciting learning activities, social events and so much more.

Throughout the year I will keep you informed of everything that's going on: my classroom plans, your child's progress and all the activities that will make this a successful—and memorable—year.

I am looking forward to sharing this year with you and your child.

Sincerely, _____ School _____

Positive News

FOR PARENTS

To: _____

Just a quick note to tell you how pleased I am that:

_____
_____
_____
_____
_____

Signed _____ Date _____

Positive News

FOR PARENTS

To: _____

Just a quick note to tell you how pleased I am that:

_____
_____
_____
_____
_____

Signed _____ Date _____

Positive News

FOR PARENTS

To: _____

Just a quick note to tell you how pleased I am that:

_____
_____
_____
_____
_____

Signed _____ Date _____

Positive News

FOR PARENTS

To: _____

Just a quick note to tell you how pleased I am that:

_____
_____
_____
_____
_____

Signed _____ Date _____

Class/Grade _____

Use this page to keep track of your use of notes, phone calls, and other means of positive communication between school and home. Circle an N for note, PC for phone call, and O for other, such as a positive conversation with a parent at a school event or in the community. Make your goal positive communication with each student's family at least once a semester.

Name	Month of _____	Month of _____	Month of _____	Month of _____	Month of _____
_____	N PC O	N PC O	N PC O	N PC O	N PC O
_____	N PC O	N PC O	N PC O	N PC O	N PC O
_____	N PC O	N PC O	N PC O	N PC O	N PC O
_____	N PC O	N PC O	N PC O	N PC O	N PC O
_____	N PC O	N PC O	N PC O	N PC O	N PC O
_____	N PC O	N PC O	N PC O	N PC O	N PC O
_____	N PC O	N PC O	N PC O	N PC O	N PC O
_____	N PC O	N PC O	N PC O	N PC O	N PC O
_____	N PC O	N PC O	N PC O	N PC O	N PC O
_____	N PC O	N PC O	N PC O	N PC O	N PC O
_____	N PC O	N PC O	N PC O	N PC O	N PC O
_____	N PC O	N PC O	N PC O	N PC O	N PC O
_____	N PC O	N PC O	N PC O	N PC O	N PC O
_____	N PC O	N PC O	N PC O	N PC O	N PC O

*For the **Initial Call** About a Problem*

Date of call: _____

Student: _____ Grade/Class: _____

Parent or Guardian: _____

Home phone: _____ Work phone: _____

Jot down points you want to cover in each of these areas during the call.

Statement of concern: _____
_____

Describe the specific problem or behavior: _____
_____

Describe steps you've taken so far: _____
_____

Get parent input on the problem: _____
_____

Record parent's comments: _____
_____

Present ideas for solutions:

   • What you'll do at school: _____
   _____

   • What you'd like parent to do at home: _____
   _____

Reassure parent problem can be solved: _____
_____

Describe the follow-up contact parent can expect: _____
_____

Notes: _____
_____
_____

Planning a Problem Phone Call *Worksheet*

For a **Follow-up Call** About a Problem

Date of call: _____

Student: _____ Grade/Class: _____

Parent or Guardian: _____

Home phone: _____ Work phone: _____

Jot down points you want to cover in each of these areas during the call.

Statement of concern about student's continuing problem: _____

_____

Describe the specific problem or behavior: _____

_____

Review what you agreed on in the previous call as ways to help solve the problem: _____

_____

_____

Get parent input on the continuing problem: _____

_____

Record parent's comments: _____

_____

Present new ideas for solutions:

 • What you'll do at school:_____

 _____

 • What you'd like parent to do at home: _____

 _____

Reassure parent, then describe next steps if problem persists: _____

_____

_____

Notes: _____

_____

_____

Planning a Problem-Solving Conference

Student: _____ Grade/Class: _____

Parent or Guardian: _____

Names of teachers/others who will attend: _____

_____

Date of conference: _____

Jot down points you want to cover in each of these areas during the conference.

Statement of concern about student's continuing problem: _____

_____

Describe the specific problem and present documentation: _____

_____

Review what has already been done to solve the problem: _____

_____

Get parent input on the problem: _____

_____

Get student input on the problem (if present) : _____

_____

Present new ideas for solutions:

- What you'll do at school: _____

    _____

- What you'd like parent to do at home: _____

    _____

Reassure parent, then describe next steps if problem persists: _____

_____

_____

Notes: _____

_____

_____

Home–School Contract

Student: _____ Grade/Class: _____

Behavior student agrees to: _____
_____

Each day _____ **follows the terms of the contract, the following positive reinforcement will be given:**

• by the undersigned teacher or team

_____
_____
_____

• by the parent

_____
_____
_____

Each day _____ **does not follow the terms of the contract, the following consequences will be given:**

• by the undersigned teacher or team

_____
_____
_____

• by the parent

_____
_____
_____

Contract is in effect from _____ **to** _____

Student's signature: _____

Parent's signature: _____

Teacher: _____ Teacher: _____

Teacher: _____ Teacher: _____

Home–School Contract
COMMUNICATION FORM

Student's Name _____ Date: _____

Dear _____

☐ Today your child behaved according to the terms of the contract. I have given the positive reinforcement that we agreed upon. Please follow through at home with your positive reinforcement, also.

☐ Today your child did not behave according to the terms of the contract. I have given the negative consequences that we agreed upon. Please follow through at home with your negative consequences, also.

Please contact me if you have any questions or if you would like to talk about the contract.

Sincerely, _____

Additional comments: _____

_____

Home–School Contract
COMMUNICATION FORM

Student's Name _____ Date: _____

Dear _____

☐ Today your child behaved according to the terms of the contract. I have given the positive reinforcement that we agreed upon. Please follow through at home with your positive reinforcement, also.

☐ Today your child did not behave according to the terms of the contract. I have given the negative consequences that we agreed upon. Please follow through at home with your negative consequences, also.

Please contact me if you have any questions or if you would like to talk about the contract.

Sincerely, _____

Additional comments: _____

_____

CHAPTER
7

Succeeding with Difficult Students

Kathy Krupar
Middle School Teacher
Cleveland, Ohio

"I believe difficult students do want to learn. By mastering techniques for working with these students, I feel better prepared to help difficult students help themselves do just that."

One of the biggest—if not *the* biggest— challenges for a teacher is students who are difficult and disruptive. They may be angry and belligerent and challenge your authority, or they may be kids who constantly act out and divert your attention from the needs of the rest of the class. But at the middle school level, the classroom dynamics of working with difficult students becomes increasingly complex. The natural tendency of early adolescents to test the limits of authority combined with the heightened need to be accepted by—or save face before—one's peers means that disruptive behavior can quickly escalate into highly charged and confrontational situations.

Your classroom discipline plan will go a long way toward helping you deal with difficult students. It provides you with a plan for how to respond when students choose to disrupt, helping you to stay calm and maintain control of yourself and your classroom. But in many cases, it won't be enough. You need to tailor your plan to meet the unique needs of chronically disruptive students. And to do that, you need to know these students and know what is at the root of their need to act out. This chapter will show you how to utilize your classroom discipline plan to succeed with difficult students.

The Importance of Building Trust

Today there is an alarming number of young adolescents who come to school angry and alienated. Often lacking the guidance and direction of a father, or a mother, or both, these students may be adrift, unwilling or unable to trust adults, to respect authority, to see a connection between an education and their success in the future. Consequently, they see little reason to follow the rules that you've established to allow you to teach and other students to learn.

While this chapter will offer a variety of strategies for working more successfully with difficult students, your first and most overriding need is to *build a relationship with each student*. You need to get to know these students as individuals, not simply as "troublemakers." Developing relationships with difficult students is key to the success of everything else you try. Building trust and communicating to the student that you really care—that you're not going to let this student continue on a course of school failure—are critical. Few students, even the most hardened, can long resist someone who demonstrates a genuine commitment to their well-being.

Tips for Establishing Trust

How can you build trust with difficult students? Review the following sections of the book for support and ideas. Reread them, thinking this time about specific students and how to put the ideas to work to help those kids:

- Reread Chapter 1, "Getting to Know the Students You Teach" with your difficult students in mind. If you haven't done so already, use the interest inventory sheets on pages 8 and 9 as a starting point for getting to know these students better.

- Think about how you can use the power of mission in Chapter 2 to help you focus your energies on the needs of difficult students.

- Use the consistency of your classroom discipline plan described in Chapters 4 and 5 to demonstrate that you are fair and impartial when giving recognition and imposing consequences. Young adolescents respect fairness. Make it clear that you have one plan for *all* students—not one for troublemakers and one for others.

- Find every opportunity to praise and positively recognize students for appropriate behavior. Offer praise quietly, one to one; reward students with positive notes and phone calls home; and motivate them with special privileges and rewards, such as a homework pass or a free ticket to a school event.

- Remember that the parents of difficult students—if properly approached—can be your ally. Review the positive-communication strategies outlined in Chapter 6 and work on building a relationship with a difficult student's family members. Use a welcome note at the start of the school year to demonstrate your interest in the student. Jump at an opportunity to praise the child to parents. They're used to being on the receiving end of complaints about their child. Imagine the difference it could make in their attitude to hear a compliment from you.

- You'll also find trust-building techniques in Chapter 9 that can bolster the self-esteem of your difficult students. Stand at the classroom door to personally greet these students; comment on clothes, music, or other interests you know they share; attend school or community events they participate in. These efforts to make positive connections with students demonstrate you care.

Sharing Through Writing

Another trust-building technique to try with difficult students is sharing a journal. Some students who won't hold a conversation face to face will communicate with you in writing. Invite students to share their thoughts, feelings, interests, concerns, hopes, and dreams in a journal. Assure the student that all communication will be kept confidential—except for any information, such as suspicion of abuse, that you're legally bound to report. Emphasize that you aren't grading the writing; this is one time when mechanics don't

matter. Then respond to the student's journal entries with comments or questions that will keep the dialogue going.

Often a difficult student's greatest need is to be recognized as a worthy individual who has the potential to be somebody and amount to something. When you demonstrate your confidence in and high expectations for these students, you offer them new incentive to succeed.

Getting to the Root of Disruptive Behavior

Research shows that difficult students act out and misbehave because of strong needs that are not adequately being met in their lives. Those needs are generally one of three types:

- **a need for attention**

- **a need for firmer limits**

- **a need for more motivation**

This means that difficult students need something from you that your other students don't. They need a teacher to recognize that real, unmet needs are prompting them to choose behaviors that are not in their best interest. They need a teacher who will help them fulfill these needs *appropriately*.

Observing the student's behavior carefully and focusing on what emotions the student triggers in you are the best ways to assess primary need. Granted, some difficult students may exhibit behaviors that signal more than one need. In such situations, focus on the strongest emotion the student triggers in you. That's your best barometer of primary need.

The Student Who Needs Attention

Difficult students who need attention signal that need through some or all of the following behaviors:

- frequently disturbs you and/or other students

- talks out in class

- makes silly noises

- constantly gets out of seat

- interrupts lessons with attention-seeking behaviors

- works only when receiving your complete attention

Emotion this student typically triggers in you: annoyance.

These behaviors are listed on an "Identifying Primary Need: Observation Checklist" on page 110. Use this sheet to help you identify attention-seeking students.

The Student Who Needs Firmer Limits

Difficult students who need firmer limits demonstrate that need through some or all of these behaviors:

- constantly challenges you or other students

- talks back to you in front of other students

- argues

- lies

- verbally or physically fights with other students

- refuses to do what is asked

Emotion this student typically triggers in you: anger.

You'll also find these behaviors listed on an "Observation Checklist" on page 111. Use this sheet to guide you in identifying students who need firmer limits.

Identifying Primary Need: *Observation Checklist*

STUDENT WHO NEEDS **ATTENTION**

Use this observation sheet to help you identify a student whose disruptions are prompted by a need for attention. Observe the student over several days. Put a check next to each problem behavior each time you observe it, and check each time the student triggers an emotional response of annoyance in you.

Student Name:_____

Class/Grade:_____ Date(s):_____

Behavior	M	T	W	Th	F
• Frequently disturbs you and/or other students					
• Talks out in class					
• Makes silly noises					
• Constantly gets out of seat					
• Interrupts lesson with attention-seeking behaviors					
• Works only when receiving your complete attention					

Times when you feel **annoyed** with student: _____

Other attention-seeking behaviors you observe: _____

Notes: _____

Identifying Primary Need: *Observation Checklist*

STUDENT WHO NEEDS **FIRMER LIMITS**

Use this observation sheet to help you identify a student whose disruptions are prompted by a need for firmer limits. Observe the student over several days. Put a check next to each problem behavior each time you observe it, and check each time the student triggers an emotional response of anger in you.

Student Name:_____

Class/Grade: _____ Date(s): _____

Behavior	M	T	W	Th	F
• Constantly challenges you and/or other students					
• Talks back to you in front of other students					
• Argues					
• Lies					
• Verbally or physically fights with other students					
• Refuses to do what is asked					

Times when you feel **angry** with student: _____

Other defiant behaviors you observe: _____

Notes: _____

The Student Who Needs Motivation

Difficult students who need motivation telegraph that need through some or all of these behaviors:

- makes excuses for why work cannot be done

- will not attempt to do academic work

- if an attempt is made, the student will give up easily

Emotion this student typically triggers in you: frustration.

Use the "Observation Checklist" on page 112 to guide you in identifying students who need more motivation.

Identifying Primary Need: *Observation Checklist*

STUDENT WHO NEEDS **MOTIVATION**

Use this observation sheet to help you identify a student whose disruptions are prompted by a need for motivation. Observe the student over several days. Put a check next to each problem behavior each time you observe it, and check each time the student triggers an emotional response of frustration in you.

Student Name:_____

Class/Grade:_____ Date(s): _____

Behavior	M	T	W	Th	F
• Makes excuses for why work cannot be done					
• Will not attempt to do academic work					
• If student tries to do work, gives up easily at slightest problem					

Times when you feel **frustrated** with student: _____

Other related behaviors you observe: _____

Notes: _____

Setting Goals for Difficult Students

Once you know a difficult student's need, you can implement more individualized techniques that will help to correct the student's behavior. Each need suggests a clear goal, an overriding aim of every interaction with the student. The goals that follow promote the greatest degree of success.

Students who need attention: Give massive amounts of positive attention for appropriate behavior.

Students who need attention will take whatever kind they can get—positive or negative. To help these students succeed, give them maximum positive attention for any and all behaviors that conform to your expectations. Your praise should be genuine, but give it frequently and freely. When you give lots of attention for appropriate behavior, and minimal attention for negative behavior, attention-seeking students learn it's in their best interest to behave.

Students who need firmer limits: Provide very firm and consistent limits.

These students want power and control. They need *very firm* and *very consistent* limits imposed in a nonconfrontational way. These students need you to be the authority figure. Always respond in a respectful manner. Even when setting limits, never respond in a way that will embarrass these students or prompt them to act tough to "save face" before their peers.

Students who need more motivation: Focus all behavioral efforts toward getting the student to do work.

Let these students know that you have confidence in their ability to be successful in your class and do the expected work. Set high expectations and share them with the student. If necessary, break assignments down to manageable parts and work through them together. Focus all corrective actions on getting these students to do the expected class work.

To assist you in setting goals for individual students, you'll find ready-to-reproduce "Setting Goals" worksheets for each type of need on pages 113-115.

Setting Goals

STUDENT WHO NEEDS **ATTENTION**

Use this sheet to help you set your goals for supporting a student whose disruptions are prompted by a need for attention.

Student Name:_____
Class/Grade:_____ Date: _____

PRIMARY GOAL:
Give massive amounts of positive attention for appropriate behavior.

Setting Goals

STUDENT WHO NEEDS **FIRMER LIMITS**

Use this sheet to help you set your goals for supporting a student whose disruptions are prompted by a need for firmer limits.

Student Name:_____
Class/Grade:_____ Date: _____

PRIMARY GOAL:
Provide very firm and consistent limits.

Setting Goals

STUDENT WHO NEEDS **MOTIVATION**

Use this sheet to help you set your goals for supporting a student who needs motivation. As you discover motivational techniques that work, note them here.

Student Name:_____
Class/Grade:_____ Date: _____

PRIMARY GOAL:
Focus all behavioral efforts toward getting the student to do work.

Forms of positive recognition that are meaningful to this student:
_____
_____
_____

Consequences that are effective with this student:
_____
_____
_____

Notes: _____
_____
_____
_____
_____

Creating a Behavior Profile

Once you've identified the student's primary need and defined your key goal, the next step is to create a behavior profile of the student. This profile will help you determine precisely when problems occur, pinpoint the exact inappropriate behaviors the student exhibits, and identify the needed behaviors. Compiling the profile also will help you have a more realistic view of the extent of the student's disruptive behavior. Often it feels as if difficult students are disruptive all the time, when actually their behavior is fairly predictable once you recognize the need that feeds it.

Think about your own difficult students, then consider if their behavior matches up with these examples.

A student who needs attention is likely to be noncompliant when he or she can't get your attention. For example:

- when you are working with a group other than the one the student is in.

- when you are working one to one with another student.

- when the student is supposed to be engaged in an independent activity.

A student who needs firm limits is likely to be noncompliant when faced with a specific direction or when placed in an unstructured situation. For example:

- during transitions, such as before class begins.

- when working in a cooperative group.

- when given a direction to follow, such as to write in response to a reading or discussion.

A student who needs motivation is likely to be noncompliant when asked to do academic work.

Use the "Behavior Profile" sheet on page 116 to begin an evaluation of each difficult student. Observe the student's behavior for a few days and note situations when the student is noncompliant.

BEHAVIOR PROFILE

Use this sheet to help you identify specific times when a student's behavior is inappropriate, the specific behaviors, and the appropriate behaviors the student needs to learn. Focus on clear, observable behaviors.

Student: _____

Class/Grade: _____ Observation Dates: _____

Student's Primary Need: ☐ Attention ☐ Firmer Limits ☐ Motivation

Times when student is noncompliant	Specific, inappropriate behaviors observed	Specific, appropriate behaviors needed

Notes: _____

Next, define the problem behaviors. Fill in the second column, listing specific, observable behaviors, such as *argues when asked to work, talks, gets out of seat, speaks without raising hand, distracts others,* and so on.

Finally, identify specific behaviors that will help the student be successful. Think through the appropriate behavior in each situation, then write your expectations in the third column.

Refer to the chart below to see how a completed behavior profile might read for a student who needs firmer limits.

By creating a behavior profile of each difficult student, you can see at a glance when the student is likely to be disruptive, what form that disruptive behavior takes, and what specific behaviors the student needs to learn. With that information at hand—and in a form that you can analyze and review—you can begin to turn around a difficult student's behavior.

Share the behavior profile with team members, too. Your individual efforts will be much more effective if carried out jointly. Try working on the same inappropriate behaviors. Use the same consistent discipline and approaches. Demonstrate that you

Student's Primary Need: ☐ Attention ☒ Firmer Limits ☐ Motivation

Times when student is noncompliant	Specific, inappropriate behaviors observed	Specific, appropriate behaviors needed
Independent seatwork	Argues when asked to work; talks; gets out of seat	Begin assignment when given direction; no talking; raise hand if help is needed
Class discussion	Interrupts others; speaks out of turn; out of seat; makes disruptive remarks	Raise hand to speak; stay seated; speak only when called upon
Group work	Out of seat; does not work cooperatively; distracts others; disruptive conversations	Stay seated; talk only about the assignment; work only on the assignment

are working together to support this student. You'll communicate the depth of your devotion—and send the message that the student can't play one teacher off another.

Teaching Appropriate Behavior

Working from the behavior profile of each difficult student, pinpoint the behavior that is most disruptive. You can't successfully teach every behavior at once, so start with the one that will make the biggest difference to you, such as behavior when you are presenting to the class. Once the student's behavior improves in this situation, you can choose another one to teach.

Most likely, the student has already been taught this set of behaviors once—when you taught specific directions for your classroom routines. Review the specific directions sheet on page 66 in Chapter 5, to be sure the directions you give now are compatible with those.

Use the "Teaching Appropriate Behavior Planning Sheet" on page 117 to help you plan how you will teach the appropriate behavior.

Talk with the student one to one, when others are not around.

"Rachel, can you please wait after class for a moment? I'd like to talk to you." Never embarrass a student in front of her peers. You'll anger the student and may increase her resolve to misbehave as a means of revenge. Have the student wait after class, or take the student into the hall to talk.

Speaking very calmly, specify the exact behaviors you expect.

"Rachel, you didn't make very good choices today about how to behave when I am presenting a lesson to the class. Is there a problem I should know about—something you would like to say about your behavior today?

Teaching Appropriate Behavior

PLANNING SHEET

This sheet offers more help in working with a difficult student. Use it to plan how you will present the behavior you expect during the classroom activity specified below. Remember, teach only one set of behaviors at a time.

Student: _____

Class/Grade: _____ Date: _____

Student's Primary Need: ☐ Attention ☐ Firmer Limits ☐ Motivation

Objective: To teach appropriate behavior for the following class activity:
_____

Specific behaviors you expect from student:
_____
_____
_____

Pointers for meeting with student:
Make notes that will help you in talking with the student.
• Meet with student privately, in the hall or after class: _____
• Review the inappropriate behavior you have observed: _____
_____
• State the appropriate behavior you expect: _____
_____
• Review or follow-up needed by this student: _____

Notes:
Write a note in your plan book to remind the student of the appropriate behavior you expect the next time you engage in this activity in class.
_____
_____
_____

Now I want you to take a moment to review the directions we have for listening to a lecture: Eyes on me, no talking, only notebook and pencil on your desk unless I specify otherwise. If you have a question or would like to speak, raise your hand and I will call on you."

Check for understanding.

"Do you have any questions about those directions? Good. Then I'll look for improvement the next time I'm presenting to the class. I'll see you tomorrow."

Naturally, you'll need to vary this approach for the age and maturity of the student. With a sixth-grader, for example, you may want to have the student repeat verbally or write down the behaviors you expect during a specific activity.

Provide ongoing support for appropriate behavior. The next time you lecture, tactfully remind the student of the behavior you expect before you begin. Speak to her quietly, or give the whole class a reminder, making eye contact with the student so that she recognizes the reminder is for her particular benefit.

Creating an Individualized Behavior Plan

Your concentrated efforts to teach appropriate behavior—using plenty of positives to reward the student's efforts and, when necessary, consequences to respond to inappropriate behavior—may be sufficient to turn around a difficult student's behavior. However, when these sustained efforts are not successful, adapt the elements of your discipline plan to meet the unique needs of this particular student. An individualized behavior plan is one more way of communicating to difficult students that you are willing to take extra steps to help them correct their behavior.

Developing the Plan

An individualized behavior plan includes:

- The specific behaviors you expect of the student.

- Meaningful consequences that you'll impose each time the student chooses to disrupt.

- Meaningful positive recognition the student receives for behaving appropriately.

The individualized plan mirrors your classroom plan in that you are stating expected behaviors, positive rewards, and consequences. The difference is that you are tailoring the plan to a student. Select rewards and consequences that will motivate this particular student to choose appropriate behavior.

Use the "Individualized Behavior Plan" sheet on page 118 and these guidelines to help you develop an individualized behavior plan.

Individualized Behavior Plan

Student: _____

Class/Grade: _____ Date: _____

This Behavior Plan is specially drawn up to meet the unique needs of

_____

By signing below, both student and teacher agree to the terms of the plan.

The Behavior Plan

Rules (specific behaviors) that _____ is expected to follow:

_____
_____
_____

Consequences that _____ will choose when not complying with the terms of the Behavior Plan.

First disruption: _____

Second disruption: _____

Positive recognition that _____ will receive when following the terms of the Behavior Plan.

_____
_____
_____

Student's signature: _____

Teacher's signature: _____

Determine the behaviors you expect from the student.

Use the student's Behavior Profile to help you select one or two behaviors to work on. Choose those that are most important to the student's success. For example, if the student is constantly interrupting and making disruptive remarks during class discussions, behaviors to target are: "Raise your hand when you want to speak or ask a question. Wait to be called on before you speak. Do not interrupt when others are talking."

Decide on meaningful consequences.

If the consequences in your behavior plan aren't working with this student, how do you come up with others? The Behavior Tracking Sheet on page 50 will come in handy here. Look for a pattern in the student's behavior. Let's say that your third consequence is staying two minutes after class, while your fourth consequence is calling parents. You notice that the student often reaches the third consequence, but never the fourth. Perhaps having parents notified is something the student wants to avoid at all costs. Make that the first consequence of a disruption in the individualized plan.

It's also possible that you'll have to come up with a totally different set of consequences from your classroom plan. You might have the student report to you during lunch, or stay after school. (Keep in mind, though, that for a student who wants attention, these would be positives. The consequences must be something the student won't like.) Just as with your classroom plan, make sure that *you* can consistently carry out each consequence.

Determine meaningful forms of positive recognition.

If your classroom positives aren't motivating this student, you need to identify privileges and rewards that will. This is another way that getting to know a student pays off. Go back to the student's interest inventory. What are his or her favorite sports, musicians, foods? You might devise a system whereby the student earns a point toward a CD of his or her favorite music. Continue to make praise and positive communication home part of your plan, but with many difficult students, praise won't be enough. They need the incentive of a tangible reward.

Present the plan to the student in a firm but empathetic way.

By your manner, assure the student that you care and that you are there to help, but that you will not allow the student's disruptive behavior to continue unchecked. It undermines your ability to teach, and even more important, it's not in the best interest of the student.

Share the plan with parents.

Even if you know the parent is not particularly attentive to the student's needs, send home a copy of the plan and review it with the parent by telephone. Use the guidelines for making a problem call to parents on page 88 of Chapter 6 to help you plan what to say. You may prefer to discuss the plan face to face with the parent during a problem-solving conference, as outlined on pages 78-82 of Chapter 6. Here are the points to cover, by phone or in person:

- Give a rationale for the individualized plan. Your goal is to help the student learn more responsible behavior that will increase his or her success in school. *Present this as a proactive step, not as a punishment.*

- Review the behaviors covered in the plan and why you've chosen to emphasize those behaviors.

- Review the consequences in the plan, in the order they will be imposed when the student chooses to disrupt. Explain your rationale for choosing those consequences.

- Explain the positive recognition you'll give when the student chooses to behave appropriately. Share your philosophy of consistent, sincere praise (particularly if you believe the student gets little praise at home). Ask the parent to support your efforts by recognizing appropriate behavior at home, too. Let the parent know that you'll use phone calls and notes to update him or her on the student's progress. (You'll find forms for sending positive notes home on page 85 of Chapter 6.)

Teaming in Support of Difficult Students

If you are part of a grade-level team, develop the "Individualized Behavior Plan: Team Plan" worksheet on page 119 together. As we've said before, you'll quadruple your efforts if each of a student's core teachers is focusing on improving the same behaviors, imposing the same consequences, and offering positive recognition that is meaningful to the student.

Individualized Behavior Plan

TEAM PLAN

Student: _____

Date: _____ Team: _____

This Behavior Plan is specially drawn up to meet the unique needs of
_____

By signing below, both the student and the team of teachers agree to the terms of the plan.

The Behavior Plan

Rules (specific behaviors) that _____ is expected to follow:
_____
_____
_____

Consequences that _____ will choose when not complying with the terms of the Behavior Plan.
First disruption: _____
Second disruption: _____

Positive recognition that _____ will receive when following the terms of the Behavior Plan.
_____
_____
_____

Student's signature: _____
Teacher: _____ Teacher: _____
Teacher: _____ Teacher: _____

Meet as a team to decide on the specifics of the plan—behaviors, consequences, and rewards—then present it to the student as a group. Emphasize that your goal is consistent support of the student. Each team member, in his or her own way, should communicate confidence in the student's ability to follow the terms of the plan and demonstrate appropriate behavior.

If you can meet with the student's parent, do so as a group. Follow the guidelines for team-parent conferences on pages 78-79 of Chapter 6. If a face-to-face meeting is not possible, designate a team spokesperson to call the parent and review the plan by phone.

During team-planning time or in informal conversation, keep one another abreast of the student's behavior in each class. Coordinate problem calls home, as well as positive notes, so that the parent is kept continually informed of the student's progress (or lack of it) but is not barraged and overwhelmed.

Techniques for Handling Disruptive Behavior

Your sustained efforts to work with difficult students—building relationships with them and tailoring your classroom plan and disciplining techniques to meet their individual needs—is sure to pay off in time. But meanwhile, there is still the behavior to contend with. Difficult students may argue, be critical, angry, verbally abusive, sullen, and rude. There will be covert and overt confrontations and disruptions to cope with. And being on the receiving end of such abuse, especially when you are working to develop a relationship with a student and make a difference in his or her life, can cause you to respond with anger and irritation. It's easy to give up on kids who don't seem willing to meet us halfway.

Don't give up. Keep the big picture in mind. For many young adolescents, their behavior has been years in the making. It won't change overnight. It may not change significantly at all this year. But if you don't take steps to help a student make better behavior choices, it may never get better. *Remember, early adolescence is the turning point.* For many young teens, it's the last best chance to make decisions that will lead to healthy, productive lives.

Planning will help you prepare for confrontations with difficult students. Here are techniques for handling disruptive students that enable you to maintain your composure and the control of your classroom.

"Moving In"

When a student continually disrupts, it's natural to get angry and to continue imposing consequences from the discipline hierarchy as the student chooses to continue to misbehave. But in the long run, you've done nothing for your relationship with that student. He or she has discovered how to "get to you."

Instead, when the student has reached the second or third consequence in your discipline hierarchy, use physical proximity to try to calm the student and stop the behavior.

Move close to the student.

Walk over to the student and get close. Speak in a quiet, firm manner. Tell the student that his or her behavior is inappropriate.

Move the student out of the classroom.

Use your own judgment, but in most cases it's best to speak to the student out of the classroom, so that the student no longer has an audience of peers. By speaking alone to the student, you're less likely to embarrass him or her and more likely to get cooperation.

Remind the student of the consequences received thus far, and what will happen next if the disruptions continue.

Stay calm and don't argue with the student. Keep your manner caring but firm: *"Chaundra, I'm concerned that your behavior today is going to result in consequences that you don't really want. You've received a warning and two consequences. One more disruption and I'll be calling your mother tonight. Do you understand?"*

By communicating to the student that this isn't a standoff—you don't want to impose consequences, you want the student to choose appropriate behavior—you demonstrate anew your commitment to this student's success.

Defusing a Covert Confrontation

A covert confrontation occurs when a student responds to you with a sneer, a dirty look, mumbles under his or her breath, or does something hostile that others in the class may be unaware of.

First, calm yourself.

To stay in control, decrease your anxiety and your body's natural inclination to react. Count to three, four, five, whatever you need. Take a deep breath. Say to yourself, "Don't get angry. This isn't about me."

Next, disengage from the student.

It's natural to respond to a challenge by exerting your authority as the teacher: *"What did I hear you say?"* or *"Don't give me that look!"* Those are fighting words to many young adolescents. By calling the class's attention to the confrontation, you'll escalate the situation. Instead, get some distance. Step away from the student. By putting some space between yourself and the student, you give the student an opening to save face, back down, and choose more appropriate behavior.

Speak to the student later.

Rude remarks and dirty looks are not behaviors you should ignore. Such signs of disrespect can lead to more blatant challenges to your authority. Speak to the student alone after class. Communicate clearly that such behavior is unacceptable.

Defusing an Overt Confrontation

Times when a student openly challenges you and verbally defies your authority require all the self-control you can muster. *Your response is critical.* You have the ability to calm a potentially violent confrontation. But if you respond in an angry or passive way, you're bound to escalate the situation. Here's how to react in an assertive way that maintains your authority and safety.

First, calm yourself.

Take a deep breath and tell yourself, "This student is angry. He wants to argue with me. I'm not going to argue. I'm not going to take this personally."

Next, give a paradoxical response.

Defuse the situation by throwing the student off guard. Respond opposite to the way the student will expect you to respond. If the student is shouting, speak softly. If the student yells louder, speak even more softly. You'll demonstrate that you're firmly in control. You are not going to be lured into an argument.

Refocus the conversation.

Acknowledge the student's feelings, then calmly restate what you need the student to do:

"Paul, I can see that you don't want to join your group. I hear that you don't want to do it. But it's your responsibility and you need to do it."

"Erica, it's clear to me that you don't want to discuss this novel with the rest of the class. But you are a member of this class. It's your responsibility to take part and contribute with the others."

Move the student away from peers.

If the student continues to be confrontational, get the student alone, such as moving out into the hall. By removing the audience of peers, the student is less compelled to act tough to save face. Continue to speak calmly, quietly, and respectfully. Repeat the specific behavior you expect from the student.

Responding to Fights

Not every confrontation will be between you and a student. You also need to know how to respond to fights between students. Your discipline plan will help you to control the environment in your classroom, so you are most likely to come upon fights in progress in the halls, bathrooms, outdoors, or other areas of the campus. No matter what your size, don't try to physically break up a fight. You could easily be hurt. Instead, follow these procedures:

First, take action to stop the punches by distracting the fighters.

Blow a whistle or issue a sharp, short command: *"Stop fighting now!"*

Disperse other students in the area.

These students may be verbally encouraging the fighters or just creating an audience. If necessary, warn students that if they don't leave the scene, they will be disciplined.

Get assistance.

Send a student to the office, blow a whistle, or give another kind of signal that other staff members will recognize as a call for help.

Remove any objects that the fighters could use as weapons.

Check also for objects they could be hurt by, such as a bench they could fall over.

In most fights between two students, those actions will allow you to assume control. However, when you come upon a fight, quickly assess the situation. The age, size, sex and number of fighters will determine whether you can stop the fight alone or will need immediate assistance from other adults. How well you know the students is also a factor. If you have a relationship with them and they respect you, you'll be able to exert more control over the situation. If you don't know the fighters, proceed with more caution.

Conducting a One-to-One Problem-Solving Conference

After a confrontation or fight, hold a problem-solving conference with the student. It's a way to express your concerns, your commitment to the student's well-being and your confidence in the student's ability to live up to your behavior and academic expectations. A student conference should always precede a problem-solving conference with the parent. (See Chapter 6 for the specifics on holding such a conference, alone or with team members.)

Use the "Problem-Solving Conference" worksheet on page 120 and these guidelines for planning and conducting a problem-solving conference with a difficult student.

PROBLEM-SOLVING CONFERENCE — WORKSHEET

Student:_____
Class/Grade:_____ Date: _____

Problem (and reasons for your concern): _____

Student input as to why problem is occurring:_____

Steps you can take to help: _____

Actions student can take to solve problem: _____

Summarize conference (restate your behavior expectations):_____

Follow-up/Comments:_____

Meet privately with the student.

Keep all discussion confidential. Meet with the student at a time and place where you won't be disturbed and others won't overhear the conversation.

State your concern.

Let the student know that you want to help. Your motive is not to embarrass or punish.

Listen to the student's point of view.

Try to find out from the student why there is a problem. Is there a change at home or a conflict with other students? Let the student take the lead in revealing information. Encourage, but don't pry.

Determine what you can do to help.

After listening to the student, decide how you can help. It might be giving the student more structure through an individualized behavior plan or involving a school counselor in working with the student.

Determine what the student can do to solve the problem.

Talk about different choices the student can make to handle the problem more successfully. If necessary, teach the appropriate behaviors to the student.

Recap by stating your behavior expectations.

Let the student know unequivocally that while you are concerned about his or her well-being, you also will not allow the inappropriate behavior to continue. Review again the appropriate behavior you expect from now on.

Using Peer Mediation to Reach Difficult Students

More and more middle schools are using peer-mediation programs to resolve conflicts among students. If you don't have such a program in your school, consider starting one.

Peer-mediation programs put more responsibility on all students to maintain a safe and comfortable environment in school. Trained peer mediators sit down with disputing students to identify the cause of a conflict and find a mutually agreeable solution. Many kids—including a lot of difficult students—are more willing to submit to a peer arbitrator than to an adult. They'll open up to peers and talk about how they feel and why they did something. Working through strong emotions and learning more appropriate responses to conflict can help a difficult student improve behavior overall.

By becoming trained peer counselors, difficult students can also assume more positive roles in school. Good mediators are leaders. You can turn around a student's negative leadership skills by giving him or her the respect and authority that comes with being a peer mediator.

What do you need to make a peer-mediation program work in your school?

- An adult who is committed to the program and will work to train and guide the peer mediators.

- A means of identifying students who will make good mediators. Many schools have teachers nominate students. You need kids who are good listeners, thinkers, and leaders, and who are mature enough to keep all mediation discussions confidential.

- A system for referring students to mediation. Both teachers and students themselves should be able to request this kind of help.

Remembering Your Mission

Difficult students are a challenge. They can drain from us the joy of teaching and the desire to continue to teach.

The techniques in this chapter do work. Planning how to respond when students disrupt, building relationships with students, and giving them consistent responses—both consequences and praise—are critical steps that will enable you to reach and teach troubled middle schoolers. Your difficult students may be your toughest, but they also have the potential to give you the greatest satisfaction. To take even a small part in changing a young adolescent's attitude toward school, learning, and life is to truly fulfill your mission as a teacher. Difficult students are not just lives you touch. They may be lives you save.

How <u>Not</u> to Become a Victim of Violence

For countless teachers in middle schools and junior highs today, there is an overriding concern that affects how they interact with students, particularly difficult or aggressive students—the fear of becoming a victim of violence.

Violence prevention is first and foremost a *school* issue. No teacher should feel alone in safeguarding his or her own person. Every teacher, administrator, and staff person in a school needs to work together to create an environment that says to students, *"We respect one another here and we respect the sanctity of our school."*

But in addition to clearly stated, consistently enforced policies that prohibit weapons, gang-style clothing, and other types of intimidating behavior or dress, these are measures individual teachers can take to communicate to students that they will not be victimized.

SAFEGUARDING YOUR SECURITY

- **Develop positive relationships with students—in school and out.**

  Research shows that students are less likely to physically attack a teacher they have a relationship with—a teacher who shows them respect and acknowledges their presence in the classroom, in the halls, in the community. Attend to students. Talk to them about their lives, as well as their homework.

- **Take preventive action through a classroom discipline plan.**

  Your classroom discipline plan helps you create a classroom environment where you are firmly in control. You know how to respond proactively to confrontations.

- **Know how to defuse a confrontation.**

  The strategies on pages 105-106 show you how to keep a confrontation from escalating out of control. Your calm and authoritative behavior in such situations speaks volumes to young teens: *I will not be a victim!*

- **Insist on backup support.**

  Lobby for school policies and physical changes to improve the safety of the campus. Advocate for a school committee to monitor school climate and a crisis-contingency plan that includes a method of communication if there is trouble. Be the squeaky wheel when it comes to school safety. Your efforts not only enhance your own security, they ensure the security of your students as well.

STUDENT WHO NEEDS **ATTENTION**

Use this observation sheet to help you identify a student whose disruptions are prompted by a need for attention. Observe the student over several days. Put a check next to each problem behavior each time you observe it, and check each time the student triggers an emotional response of annoyance in you.

Student Name: _____

Class/Grade: _____ Date(s): _____

Behavior	M	T	W	Th	F
• Frequently disturbs you and/or other students					
• Talks out in class					
• Makes silly noises					
• Constantly gets out of seat					
• Interrupts lesson with attention-seeking behaviors					
• Works only when receiving your complete attention					

Times when you feel **annoyed** with student: _____

_____

Other attention-seeking behaviors you observe: _____

_____

_____

Notes: _____

_____

_____

_____

STUDENT WHO NEEDS **FIRMER LIMITS**

Use this observation sheet to help you identify a student whose disruptions are prompted by a need for firmer limits. Observe the student over several days. Put a check next to each problem behavior each time you observe it, and check each time the student triggers an emotional response of anger in you.

Student Name: _____

Class/Grade: _____ Date(s): _____

Behavior	**M**	**T**	**W**	**Th**	**F**
• Constantly challenges you and/or other students					
• Talks back to you in front of other students					
• Argues					
• Lies					
• Verbally or physically fights with other students					
• Refuses to do what is asked					

Times when you feel **angry** with student: _____

_____

Other defiant behaviors you observe: _____

_____

_____

_____

Notes: _____

_____

_____

_____

_____

STUDENT WHO NEEDS **MOTIVATION**

Use this observation sheet to help you identify a student whose disruptions are prompted by a need for motivation. Observe the student over several days. Put a check next to each problem behavior each time you observe it, and check each time the student triggers an emotional response of frustration in you.

Student Name: _____

Class/Grade: _____ Date(s): _____

Behavior	M	T	W	Th	F
• Makes excuses for why work cannot be done					
• Will not attempt to do academic work					
• If student tries to do work, gives up easily at slightest problem					

Times when you feel **frustrated** with student: _____

_____

Other related behaviors you observe: _____

_____

_____

Notes: _____

_____

_____

_____

STUDENT WHO NEEDS **ATTENTION**

Use this sheet to help you set your goals for supporting a student whose disruptions are prompted by a need for attention.

Student Name: _____

Class/Grade: _____ Date: _____

PRIMARY GOAL:

Give massive amounts of positive attention for appropriate behavior.

Forms of positive recognition that are meaningful to this student:

_____

_____

_____

_____

Consequences that are effective with this student:

_____

_____

_____

_____

Notes: _____

_____

_____

_____

_____

STUDENT WHO NEEDS **FIRMER LIMITS**

Use this sheet to help you set your goals for supporting a student whose disruptions are prompted by a need for firmer limits.

Student Name: _____

Class/Grade: _____ Date: _____

PRIMARY GOAL:

Provide very firm and consistent limits.

Forms of positive recognition that are meaningful to this student:

_____

_____

_____

_____

Consequences that are effective with this student:

_____

_____

_____

_____

Notes: _____

_____

_____

_____

_____

STUDENT WHO NEEDS **MOTIVATION**

Use this sheet to help you set your goals for supporting a student who needs motivation. As you discover motivational techniques that work, note them here.

Student Name: _____

Class/Grade: _____ Date: _____

PRIMARY GOAL:

Focus all behavioral efforts toward getting the student to do work.

Forms of positive recognition that are meaningful to this student:

_____

_____

_____

_____

Consequences that are effective with this student:

_____

_____

_____

_____

Notes: _____

_____

_____

_____

_____

BEHAVIOR PROFILE

Use this sheet to help you identify specific times when a student's behavior is inappropriate, the specific behaviors, and the appropriate behaviors the student needs to learn. Focus on clear, observable behaviors.

Student: _____

Class/Grade: _____ Observation Dates: _____

Student's Primary Need: ☐ Attention ☐ Firmer Limits ☐ Motivation

Times when student is noncompliant	Specific, inappropriate behaviors observed	Specific, appropriate behaviors needed
_____	_____	_____
_____	_____	_____
_____	_____	_____
_____	_____	_____
_____	_____	_____
_____	_____	_____
_____	_____	_____
_____	_____	_____
_____	_____	_____
_____	_____	_____
_____	_____	_____
_____	_____	_____
_____	_____	_____
_____	_____	_____
_____	_____	_____
_____	_____	_____
_____	_____	_____

Notes: _____
_____
_____

This sheet offers more help in working with a difficult student. Use it to plan how you will present the behavior you expect during the classroom activity specified below. Remember, teach only one set of behaviors at a time.

Student: _____

Class/Grade: _____ **Date:** _____

Student's Primary Need: ☐ Attention ☐ Firmer Limits ☐ Motivation

Objective: To teach appropriate behavior for the following class activity:

_____

Specific behaviors you expect from student:

_____

_____

_____

Pointers for meeting with student:
Make notes that will help you in talking with the student.

• Meet with student privately, in the hall or after class: _____

• Review the inappropriate behavior you have observed: _____

_____

• State the appropriate behavior you expect: _____

_____

• Review or follow-up needed by this student: _____

_____

Notes:
Write a note in your plan book to remind the student of the appropriate behavior you expect the next time you engage in this activity in class.

_____

_____

_____

Individualized Behavior Plan

Student: _____

Class/Grade: _____ **Date:** _____

This Behavior Plan is specially drawn up to meet the unique needs of

_____

By signing below, both student and teacher agree to the terms of the plan.

The Behavior Plan

Rules (specific behaviors) that _____ is expected to follow:

_____

_____

_____

Consequences that _____ will choose when not complying with the terms of the Behavior Plan.

First disruption: _____

Second disruption: _____

Positive recognition that _____ will receive when following the terms of the Behavior Plan.

_____

_____

_____

Student's signature: _____

Teacher's signature: _____

Individualized Behavior Plan

TEAM PLAN

Student: _____

Date: _____ **Team:** _____

This Behavior Plan is specially drawn up to meet the unique needs of

_____

By signing below, both the student and the team of teachers agree to the terms of the plan.

The Behavior Plan

Rules (specific behaviors) that _____ is expected to follow:

_____

_____

_____

Consequences that _____ will choose when not complying with the terms of the Behavior Plan.

First disruption: _____

Second disruption: _____

Positive recognition that _____ will receive when following the terms of the Behavior Plan.

_____

_____

_____

Student's signature: _____

Teacher: _____ Teacher: _____

Teacher: _____ Teacher: _____

PROBLEM-SOLVING CONFERENCE

Student: _____

Class/Grade: _____ Date: _____

Problem (and reasons for your concern): _____
_____
_____

Student input as to why problem is occurring: _____
_____
_____

Steps you can take to help: _____
_____
_____

Actions student can take to solve problem: _____
_____
_____

Summarize conference (restate your behavior expectations): _____
_____
_____

Follow-up/Comments: _____
_____
_____

Managing Homework Issues With Ease

Kimberly Kleinfeld
Middle School Teacher
Okeana, Ohio

"By becoming a more assertive teacher, I'm not only more effective with discipline issues, I've acquired other management techniques that make teaching easier and less stressful."

One of the benefits of becoming an assertive teacher, one who is better able to manage the behavior in your classroom, is that you also become better at managing other learning activities and routines. At the top of the list is homework.

Contrary to what we may feel as teachers, homework isn't a behavior issue. There can be legitimate reasons why a student doesn't complete a given assignment. That's why we don't recommend including rules related to homework in your classroom discipline plan. Those rules are meant to be observable in-class behaviors. But because homework issues can be so frustrating, teachers end up treating them like behavior problems, using their classroom plan—a system already in place—to manage homework.

That's not to say homework isn't important. It is a critical management issue, particularly in the middle school years. Many students who do not do homework may be students who have behavior problems or may be headed for them.

On the positive side—and one of the reasons for including this chapter in a book on behavior—a student who learns to be responsible for doing homework has a better chance of transferring that sense of responsibility into areas of behavior. Also, for middle-level students, learning good homework skills prepares them for the heavier homework load they'll experience in high school.

Just as managing behavior requires its own distinct set of skills for both teacher and students to master, so does homework. This chapter provides specific strategies for teaching middle school students responsible homework habits. There's also guidance for communicating with parents about this important issue. You know that in many homes, the "Did you do your homework?" query is often the start of a nightly battle. Sharing tips and techniques for managing homework is sure to be welcomed by parents—and even by students themselves!

Setting and Communicating Your Homework Policy

Teaching responsible homework habits begins by communicating to students and parents your expectations regarding homework. Be proactive. Don't wait for a problem to surface before addressing the how's and why's of homework. Create a homework policy that clarifies the value of homework and specifies what you expect of students and what homework support you would like from parents. Then share your policy with every class and every family on the first day of school.

Formulating a Homework Policy

Use the "Homework Policy" worksheet on page 131 and the guidelines that follow to help you develop your homework policy.

HOMEWORK POLICY

WORKSHEET

Use this sheet to help you develop your homework policy. Share the finished policy with students and parents.

Your rationale for assigning homework: _____

Types of homework you assign: _____

Amount and frequency of homework: _____

What you expect from students in completing homework:
◆ _____
◆ _____
◆ _____
◆ _____
◆ _____

Your homework record-keeping system: _____

How homework factors in students' overall grade: _____

Ways you reward good homework skills: _____

Homework support you expect from parents:
◆ _____
◆ _____
◆ _____
◆ _____

Explain your rationale for assigning homework.

This may seem unnecessary for middle school students, but don't assume they know why teachers give homework. Many students are sure to view it as simply a burden, even a kind of punishment. Help students understand that you have a clear purpose for assigning homework.

Explain the value of homework in the curriculum— as a means of reinforcing skills and content presented in class. Homework also helps students learn to work independently and take responsibility for their own learning. Point out that those skills will serve students in high school, in education or training they pursue after graduation, and in the world of work.

Review the types of homework you assign.

Different types of homework meet different learning needs. Share with students your expectations—a set of math problems assigned daily, a writing assignment or science lab report due each week, an in-depth report or project due at the completion of a unit. Cover the range and variety of homework assignments in your written policy.

Review the amount and frequency of homework.

Will you give homework every night? How long should it take a student to complete a typical assignment? You'll need to average and estimate here, but give students and parents an idea of how much homework to expect.

Share your expectations for completing homework.

Here are typical expectations to include:

- Students will do homework on their own and to the best of their ability.

- Students are expected to finish all assignments completely, unless there are special circumstances.

- In cases where a student does not understand an assignment and cannot complete it, student must (1) demonstrate that he or she made an honest attempt to do homework; (2) be able to explain what he or she does not understand; (3) make up the homework assignment once the problem is solved.

- Turn in homework on the due date assigned.

- Students are responsible for making up homework missed during an absence.

Explain your homework record-keeping system.

Reinforce the importance of homework by sharing with students your method for recording each assignment. The "Homework Record-Keeping Sheet" on page 132 is one way of tracking individual assignments. For each student, there's a place to note if assignment is complete (or incomplete), ready on time (or late), grade (if any), and comments.

HOMEWORK RECORD-KEEPING SHEET				
Assignment:				
Date Given: _____ Date Due: _____ Class/Period: _____				
Student	Homework Ready On Time or Late	Complete or Incomplete	Grade	Comments

Explain how homework will factor in students' overall grade.

Use your grading policies to underscore the importance of doing homework with care.

Share ways you will positively reinforce good homework skills.

Extend your focus on rewarding appropriate behavior by recognizing students for demonstrating good homework skills. Choose rewards that are meaningful to your students, such as praise, positive notes home, or a "homework pass" giving students a night or weekend off from homework.

Clarify what homework support you expect from parents.

Just as parent support of your discipline plan is vital, support of your homework policy is, too. Include guidelines to help parents understand the specifics of their role. For example, ask parents to:

- create a comfortable, quiet study area at home where their young adolescent can do homework.

- offer support but do not do the homework for their child.

- monitor to be sure their child completes homework each night.

- contact you if their child seems to have consistent problems understanding and finishing homework assignments.

Sharing the Policy

Make a copy of your policy to give to each student. Review it with each class, and check for understanding to be sure your homework expectations are clear to every student.

Send the policy home for student and parent to review together. Include a tear-off form, asking for the parent's signature, as a record that each parent is aware of your homework policy. Leave a space

for parents to comment or raise questions about the policy, and be sure to respond to each comment or query promptly. Your willingness to seek parent input and encourage an ongoing dialogue sets a positive tone for home-school relations.

Give a copy of the homework policy to your administrator. It's a professional courtesy that can pay off in the event a parent takes issue with your policy.

Coordinating Homework Among the Team

Share your homework policy with your grade-level colleagues or team members. Uniform homework policies are another way the team can demonstrate solidarity. And by coordinating assignments, you can avoid overloading students during the week or weekend.

By sharing homework plans and policies, and showing students that their teachers communicate about homework, the team demonstrates their respect for one another's subjects. That collaborative, cooperative stance also tells students that the team's first priority is working together to assure students' success.

Teaching Students to Take Responsibility for Homework

Middle school students are at an age when they can and need to take responsibility for their own learning. Build on early adolescents' strong urge to "take charge" in other areas of their lives by promoting the idea of taking charge of schoolwork, too. And assist students by teaching them homework study skills they can draw on for the rest of their school years.

Brainstorming Ways to Take Charge of Homework

Discuss with students ways they can "take charge" of homework. These include:

- making sure they understand all homework assignments and taking the initiative to get clarification if they don't.

- taking all necessary books and materials home to complete assignments.

- doing homework oneself.

- finding a quiet place at home or in another setting, such as the school or public library, that's conducive to study.

- completing assignments on time.

- doing one's best.

Invite students to share common problems they have in doing homework, such as not understanding the assignment. Then brainstorm solutions to this problem. For example:

- Check assignment before leaving class.

- Ask teacher for clarification.

- Call a friend.

- Ask parent for help.

Share with students the "Study Snags & Solutions" worksheet on page 133. As homework, ask students to complete the sheet, brainstorming homework problems and possible solutions. Tell kids to leave the "Evaluation" lines for each problem blank for now.

Collect students' worksheets to check for homework problems and solutions they identify. Their responses will give you insights into the type and amount of homework support they need from you.

Return the worksheets to students. Over the next few weeks, have kids refer to their Study Snags & Solutions sheets when they have a homework

Study Snags & Solutions

You know that doing homework isn't always smooth sailing. Different kinds of problems can trip you up and slow you down in completing homework on time and in doing the best job you can.

Use this worksheet to help you identify your biggest homework problems. For each problem, brainstorm as many solutions as you can think of. Then try each solution to find the one that works best for you.

Homework Problem #1:_____

Possible Solutions:_____

Evaluation — the solution that works best:_____

Homework Problem #2:_____

Possible Solutions:_____

Evaluation — the solution that works best:_____

Homework Problem #3:_____

Possible Solutions:_____

Evaluation — the solution that works best:_____

problem and try their own solutions. When kids are satisfied that they've found the best solution to a homework problem, have them describe it in the "Evaluation" section. Ask students to share their best homework solutions with the class.

Creating a Homework Study Area

As you review students' Study Snags & Solutions homework sheets, watch for references to problems related to where students do homework. A common problem for some students, especially at this age, is doing homework in front of the television or while listening to music. While some home environments are genuinely not conducive to study, in many more situations, students who are distracted by television or music don't take the initiative to find a quiet place to work at home. Help students recognize that setting up a study area is part of taking responsibility for homework.

Designing the Ideal Study Area

Discuss with students these guidelines for creating a study area:

- **A study area can be anywhere**—kitchen, bedroom, living room, den. It doesn't matter where it is, as long as the student can concentrate there. For many students, it should be quiet and away from distractions, such as the television, VCR, radio, stereo and family phone. Other students may be able to study successfully while listening to music or hearing other background noise. Each student should determine in what kind of atmosphere he or she concentrates best.

- **A study area should be comfortable,** a place where the student feels at ease. Adding pillows, colorful posters, or pictures of family, friends or pets are all ways to personalize a study area.

- **A study area should be functional.** A table or desk, comfortable chair and good light are essential. In addition, the study area should have all of the necessary homework tools—paper (lined and unlined), pens, pencils, dictionary and thesaurus. Other helpful but nonessential tools include an encyclopedia and a typewriter or computer and printer.

Share with students the sheets on page 134 and 135, "Designing Your Ideal Study Area" and "Creating a Homework Survival Kit," and have them create a floor plan of their ideal study area and a Homework Survival Kit list of supplies they need. Then encourage students to sit down with parents to work out logistics for setting up this area at home and getting the needed materials.

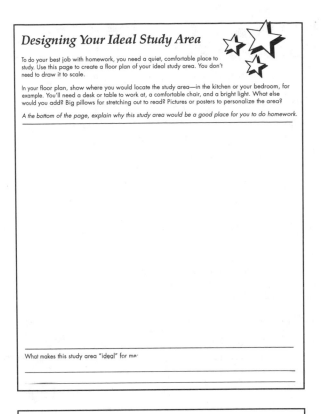

Designing Your Ideal Study Area

To do your best job with homework, you need a quiet, comfortable place to study. Use this page to create a floor plan of your ideal study area. You don't need to draw it to scale.

In your floor plan, show where you would locate the study area—in the kitchen or your bedroom, for example. You'll need a desk or table to work at, a comfortable chair, and a bright light. What else would you add? Big pillows for stretching out to read? Pictures or posters to personalize the area?

A the bottom of the page, explain why this study area would be a good place for you to do homework.

What makes this study area "ideal" for me:

CREATING A
Homework Survival Kit

My Homework Survival Kit

Must have:

Imagine you're marooned—in your room! You have a page of math problems to do, your science lab report to complete, and a reaction to the novel the class finished today to write. Do you have all of the necessary supplies at hand to make it through this ordeal? Is your Homework Survival Kit at the ready?

A Homework Survival Kit is made up of the tools and materials you need do your typical homework assignments. Use the lines on this sheet to brainstorm all of the items you would put in your Homework Survival Kit. Separate the items into two lists, "must have" (can't do homework without these things) and "great to have" (make doing homework easier, but not essential). Share your Kit lists with your family.

Great to have:

Getting Organized for Homework

One of the biggest challenges for many middle school students is keeping track of homework assignments from several teachers. Use the ideas that follow to help your middle school students get organized for homework. The time you spend now on encouraging these skills will pay off all year long!

Getting Organized with Assignment Sheets

Invite volunteers to share how they keep track of homework assignments during the day. Some students may have good systems from which peers can benefit. Then pass out the "Homework Assignments" sheet on page 136. Provide a stapler for securing it to the front of a notebook or folder. Or have students slip the sheet inside a notebook pocket.

Homework ASSIGNMENTS

Week of_____ Name_____

Use this sheet to help you keep track of homework assignments and when each is due.

Math:
_____
_____
_____
Due _____

English:
_____
_____
_____
Due _____

Science:
_____
_____
_____
Due _____

Social Studies:
_____
_____
_____
Due _____

Other: _____
_____
_____
Due _____

Other: _____
_____
_____
Due _____

Review with students tips for using this weekly planner to record homework assignments in each class. Ask students for their ideas, too. Here are some points to discuss:

- Take time to record a homework assignment before leaving class. Don't rely on a friend's understanding or your memory of what the assignment was.

- If you're not sure about an assignment, see the teacher before the day is out. Know what you need to do before you leave school.

- Get in the habit of noting on the assignment sheet when homework is due. It's easy to forget about an assignment that's not due for several days and then have to do all the work in one evening.

- Check your assignment sheet before you leave school, to be sure you take home all books and materials you need that night.

Point out that having all assignments in one place also allows students to keep track of the amount of homework they're getting in one day. If a student has a family or school event on a school night, he or she can anticipate in advance if completing homework may be a problem and present the situation to the teacher when the homework is assigned, rather than when it's due.

Scheduling Homework Time

Point out that just as students plan for school, sports and social time, they need to plan for homework, too. Blocking out a daily study period helps ensure that students have adequate time to do homework with care.

DAILY PLANNER Name _____

Use this page to block out all of your daily activities—school; classes, sports, and chores after school; and your own time to relax. Then work within your schedule to block out a **daily homework time** Setting aside a specific time to do homework is the best way to be sure you will get it done and do the best job you can.

	Monday	Tuesday	Wednesday	Thursday	Friday
8:00					
8:30					
9:00					
9:30					
10:00					
10:30					
11:00					
11:30					
12:00					
12:30					
1:00					
1:30					
2:00					
2:30					
3:00					
3:30					
4:00					
4:30					
5:00					
5:30					
6:00					
6:30					
7:00					
7:30					
8:00					
8:30					
9:00					
9:30					
10:00					
10:30					
11:00					

Pass out the "Daily Planner" worksheet on page 137 and ask students to fill it in. For example, students might block out 8:00 A.M. to 3:00 P.M. as school hours. From 3:00 P.M. to 4:30 P.M. on Tuesday and Thursday a student might have ball practice. Some students may be in charge of younger siblings after school, so that 3:30 P.M. to 6:00 P.M. is taken up with baby-sitting responsibilities.

Encourage students to be honest about how they spend their time. If they watch TV for three hours after school, they should record that. Some kids need a chance to relax after school before tackling homework; others feed off the adrenaline of the school day and do better completing homework immediately after school. Students should listen to their own body rhythms and schedule homework for those times when they are most alert and able to do their best work.

Focusing on the unscheduled time on their sheets, ask students to reserve one to two study hours each day—whatever is realistic for the volume of homework they typically receive. If some students have difficulty finding a reasonable time for homework—say before 8:00 P.M.—sit down with each to see how to alter the daily schedule to make room for study. For example, instead of watching TV until dinnertime, a student might watch TV for an hour, then devote an hour to homework. In cases where too many activities—sports, clubs and classes—or too many domestic responsibilities are cutting into a student's homework time, discuss the student's schedule with the parent, in person or by telephone.

Following Up

Ask students to stick to their scheduled study times for a few weeks, then discuss the results. Did students find that setting a time for homework helped them approach assignments more responsibly? Did they do a better job, because they were working at the hours when they felt most alert?

Have students review their Study Snags & Solutions worksheets and check for problems related to finding time for homework. Has their new study schedule solved these or other concerns?

Watch also for problems that students uncover as they become more aware of the amount of time they spend on homework. If some students are spending hours on homework each night, that's a signal they're struggling. Take steps to get these students the help they need.

When Students Don't Complete Homework...

The strategies in this chapter will make a difference with most of your students. But there will always be some kids who won't complete homework assignments. Getting to know your students will help you anticipate which students may have the greatest difficulty accepting this responsibility, be it because of immaturity, lack of motivation, lack of supervision and direction at home, or learning problems.

When a student fails to complete homework, ask yourself:

- Did I thoroughly explain the assignment?

- Does the student have the skills to complete it? Could this student have a learning disability that's been undetected?

- Is there a change in the home environment that makes study and concentration difficult?

- Do I collect and provide feedback on homework on a regular basis—or do I too often fail to follow up on assignments, sending mixed messages about the importance of doing homework?

Turn to Chapter 7 for ideas for working with students whose poor homework record—along with inappropriate classroom behavior—stems from a need for attention, firmer limits, or motivation. When homework problems persist, you may need to involve the parent in finding solutions. Use the guidelines in Chapter 6 for working through a problem call, page 87, or conducting a problem-solving conference, page 89.

Accentuate the Positive

Finally, evaluate your own responses to homework. Do you acknowledge and reward appropriate homework skills? Remember, assertive teachers let students know exactly what they expect, but they also use positive recognition to motivate students to meet their expectations. If you need ideas for homework positives, turn to Chapter 9. You'll find ideas and guidelines for accentuating the positive— in early adolescents' homework skills, behavior, and attitude toward school.

Use this sheet to help you develop your homework policy. Share the finished policy with students and parents.

Your rationale for assigning homework: _____

_____

Types of homework you assign: _____

_____

Amount and frequency of homework: _____

_____

What you expect from students in completing homework:

◆ _____

◆ _____

◆ _____

◆ _____

◆ _____

Your homework record-keeping system: _____

_____

How homework factors in students' overall grade: _____

_____

Ways you reward good homework skills: _____

_____

Homework support you expect from parents:

◆ _____

◆ _____

◆ _____

◆ _____

HOMEWORK RECORD-KEEPING SHEET

Assignment: _____

Date Given: _____ **Date Due:** _____ **Class/Period:** _____

Student	Homework Ready On Time or Late	Complete or Incomplete	Grade	Comments

Study Snags & Solutions

You know that doing homework isn't always smooth sailing. Different kinds of problems can trip you up and slow you down in completing homework on time and in doing the best job you can.

Use this worksheet to help you identify your biggest homework problems. For each problem, brainstorm as many solutions as you can think of. Then try each solution to find the one that works best for you.

Homework Problem #1: _____

_____

Possible Solutions: _____

_____

Evaluation—the solution that works best: _____

_____

Homework Problem #2: _____

_____

Possible Solutions: _____

_____

Evaluation—the solution that works best: _____

_____

Homework Problem #3: _____

_____

Possible Solutions: _____

_____

Evaluation—the solution that works best: _____

_____

Designing Your Ideal Study Area

To do your best job with homework, you need a quiet, comfortable place to study. Use this page to create a floor plan of your ideal study area. You don't need to draw it to scale.

In your floor plan, show where you would locate the study area—in the kitchen or your bedroom, for example. You'll need a desk or table to work at, a comfortable chair, and a bright light. What else would you add? Big pillows for stretching out to read? Pictures or posters to personalize the area?

A the bottom of the page, explain why this study area would be a good place for you to do homework.

What makes this study area "ideal" for me: _____

_____

_____

CREATING A
Homework Survival Kit

Imagine you're marooned—in your room! You have a page of math problems to do, your science lab report to complete, and a reaction to the novel the class finished today to write. Do you have all of the necessary supplies at hand to make it through this ordeal? Is your Homework Survival Kit at the ready?

A Homework Survival Kit is made up of the tools and materials you need do your typical homework assignments. Use the lines on this sheet to brainstorm all of the items you would put in your Homework Survival Kit. Separate the items into two lists, "must have" (can't do homework without these things) and "great to have" (make doing homework easier, but not essential). Share your Kit lists with your family.

My Homework Survival Kit

Must have:

_____

_____

_____

_____

_____

_____

_____

_____

_____

_____

_____

_____

_____

Great to have:

_____

_____

_____

_____

_____

_____

_____

_____

Homework ASSIGNMENTS

Week of_____ **Name**_____

Use this sheet to help you keep track of homework assignments and when each is due.

Math:

_____
_____
_____

Due_____

English:

_____
_____
_____

Due_____

Science:

_____
_____
_____

Due_____

Social Studies:

_____
_____
_____

Due_____

Other:_____

_____
_____

Due_____

Other:_____

_____
_____

Due_____

DAILY PLANNER

Name _____

Use this page to block out all of your daily activities—school; classes, sports, and chores after school; and your own time to relax. Then work within your schedule to block out a **daily homework time**. Setting aside a specific time to do homework is the best way to be sure you will get it done and do the best job you can.

	Monday	**Tuesday**	**Wednesday**	**Thursday**	**Friday**
8:00					
8:30					
9:00					
9:30					
10:00					
10:30					
11:00					
11:30					
12:00					
12:30					
1:00					
1:30					
2:00					
2:30					
3:00					
3:30					
4:00					
4:30					
5:00					
5:30					
6:00					
6:30					
7:00					
7:30					
8:00					
8:30					
9:00					
9:30					
10:00					
10:30					
11:00					

Accentuate the Positive!

Steve Saines
Middle School Teacher
Chicago, Illinois

"Lee Canter's ideas have helped me feel prepared to succeed in the year to come. Every teacher can benefit from his approach to classroom management."

f there is one word that characterizes the Lee Canter approach to behavior management, it is *positive*. Discipline doesn't have to be harsh and punitive to be effective. In fact, discipline that "punishes" kids for misbehavior is far less effective than discipline that rewards students for appropriate behavior. Negative consequences *stop* inappropriate behavior. Positive rewards have the power to *change* behavior. A discipline plan that focuses on misbehavior diverts all of your attention to the kids who are acting out. A discipline plan that acknowledges and rewards positive behavior lets you give equal time to those students who, by their behavior, communicate that they are ready to learn.

Positive recognition is the cornerstone of successful behavior management in the middle school. In previous chapters, we've provided guidelines for incorporating positive recognition into your classroom discipline plan. This last chapter is filled with more ideas and strategies to help you "accentuate the positive"—in your approach to students, in their behavior, in your classroom, in your school.

A Positive Approach Begins with You

In the pages that follow you'll find ideas for special privileges, rewards, and other ways to acknowledge student behavior. But the most important means you have of providing your students with the incentive to do well and get along in your classroom is *you*—your attitude, your interest, your clear support of students. It all goes back to building positive relationships with students and getting to know them as individuals.

Here are ways to show students that you care—that you're on their side, that you want them to succeed in your subject, in your classroom, in *life*. These ideas don't take a great deal of time; some don't even take a lot of extra effort. But they demonstrate how to use every opportunity to accentuate the positive in your interactions with students.

Greet Students at the Classroom Door

Here's the most effective way to ensure that you have positive contact with every student, every day. Stand at the door as students enter the classroom. Say hello to each. Notice new hair styles and new clothing. Congratulate athletes (male and female) on a winning game or demonstration of good sportsmanship. Comment on a good test score, good paper, interesting insights in a class discussion the previous day. Mention a TV show you know kids like to watch. In short, make a personal connection with each student. Your remarks don't have to be lengthy, and the more spontaneous, the better, but show each student that you acknowledge his or her presence in your classroom. Communicate to your students that you are in the business of teaching *individuals*, not English or math or science. Your upbeat and welcoming posture also starts the class on a positive note.

Give Students Your Time

For some kids, the chance to spend time with you— such as lunch together or a few minutes after school talking in your classroom—can be a privilege in itself. Take your cues from students and listen and watch in particular for those who lack the guidance and support of a responsible adult in their lives. Your open, caring manner and willingness to give of your time tells students that you are behind them and are committed to their success.

Acknowledge Events in Your Students' Lives

If a student is sick, telephone to see how he or she is doing. If a student experiences a death in the family or other loss, or a cause for special celebration, such as a sibling who wins a sports award or a college scholarship, show your concern or your pleasure.

Call the student at home, write a note or just make a point of speaking to the student at school. Demonstrate to students that your interest in their success and well-being extends beyond a particular subject or period a day.

Use the Phone to Reach Out and Touch a Student

We've talked about the value of calling parents at home to share good news about a student's performance or to involve the parent in working through a problem. But don't forget to use the phone to reach out to students as well. After a difficult day, call a student and express your concern as well as your confidence that, together, you can work through the problem, be it academic or behavioral. The point of the call is not to apologize for consequences imposed or other discipline actions. It's to reinforce the message that your first goal is to help this student do well in your classroom. It's not always possible to adequately send that message at school. And it can have twice the meaning when it's received through a personal call to the student at home.

Equally important, when a student has a particularly good day, especially a student who is one of your "difficult" kids or one who rarely speaks out or excels in your class, call to tell the student you were pleased with his or her performance. This is especially effective with students who would be embarrassed to receive such praise in front of peers.

The Value of Positive Support

Despite their outward efforts to blend in and be part of the group, you know that young adolescents want to be noticed. By acknowledging each student, you help each to feel important and accepted in your classroom. For young adolescents who often struggle with feelings of low self-esteem, your attitude is a self-concept booster. And each of these ideas—from greeting students at the door, to spending time with them, to calling kids at home—enables you to work around the "no-praise policy" of many young teens. You can quietly acknowledge students' appropriate behavior one to one.

Naturally, you have to work out the logistics of how much time you can devote to your students and still meet other responsibilities to your job, your family, your personal life. But in most cases, we're talking about a few extra minutes here and there. Not every student will need as much care and attention as others. Yet, by communicating through your manner that you genuinely like this crazy age called early adolescence, that your smile and listening ear are available to any student who needs them, you create a positive atmosphere around you. When you reach out to your students, you make it easier for kids to reach out to you, to respect you and your rules, to make an effort in your classroom.

Using Positive Recognition to Promote Positive Behavior

You give dozens of directions in each class period. Whom do you focus on when you give directives— the students who are meeting your expectations or the ones who are not?

When we focus on the students who aren't doing what they should be doing, we create a negative atmosphere. The air is filled with negative words— *don't* talk; *stop* fooling around. Kids whose disruptive behavior is motivated by a need for power enjoy these face-offs. Kids who disrupt from a need for attention get exactly what they're looking for—attention. In the meantime, the students who follow your directions are lost in the running battles around them, yet they feel the tension and the negativity all the same.

Here's the perfect opportunity to accentuate the positive. When you give a direction, get in the habit of looking for the students who are doing what you've asked them to do. Focus first on who is behaving appropriately. Then use their positive behavior to redirect inappropriate behavior through positive repetition.

Tips on Using Positive Repetition

Here's how to use this technique effectively:

- Give a direction.

- Immediately look for at least two students who are following the direction.

- Acknowledge those students and restate the direction they are following.

- With young adolescents, who may be embarrassed by such public praise, award points toward a classwide privilege for each student who is acknowledged. (For guidelines in setting up a classwide reward system, turn to Chapter 4, pages 39–40, and page 146 in this chapter.)

- Use positive repetition frequently, especially at the start of the year, to help students remember the specific behaviors you expect for each class routine.

Scanning in Small-Group Settings

Cooperative-group work can be among the most difficult to manage. Scanning offers a way of combining positive repetition and praise. As you circulate among different groups, working with each, look up every few minutes and scan the room, checking to see if all groups are on task. As you notice a group of students who are working well together, recognize their behavior: "*Matt, Li, Kaitlin, Florenzio, and Flan, I like the way you are working together. That's a point for the class toward pizza. Thank you!*" At the same time, other students get the message that you are aware of the behavior throughout the room.

Use scanning more frequently at the beginning of the year, to help remind students of what behavior you expect, and with group work, to reinforce the message that group time is not for socializing. But no matter how often or when you use scanning, it tells students that you always know what's going on in the classroom—and that your focus is on positive behavior first!

Circulating (and Praising) Around the Room

In earlier chapters we made the point that moving purposefully around the room is an effective way to communicate a feeling of control in the classroom and to redirect students who may be off task but not disruptive. Looked at another way, it's also an excellent opportunity to praise students' positive behavior in the quiet, less public way that most early adolescents prefer.

As you lecture, moderate a class discussion or oversee independent work, move about the classroom. Look for opportunities to acknowledge appropriate behavior. It might be a smile and a nod to one student, a pat on the shoulder for another. Lean down and quietly praise a student who has been working intently on a writing assignment—and perhaps ignoring some inappropriate whispering around him.

If you stay put at the front of the classroom, or sit grading papers at your desk when students are working in groups or independently, you miss a golden opportunity to deliver praise and positive support.

Gold-Star Ideas for Positive Support

Words of praise that recognize and reinforce appropriate behavior are your most effective means of encouraging more of the same. Praise can be given any time, anywhere, to as many students who deserve it, with no cost to you. And praise that's genuine and specific—that tells students exactly what they've done right—and delivered in simple, casual language, will be received with pleasure by the great majority of students.

All that aside, there are times when praise is not the best motivator in a particular situation. For some middle-schoolers, special privileges and rewards, coupled with quiet praise or positive notes home, provide a powerful combination that can help to turn around negative attitudes and behavior.

Many middle school teachers prefer to draw ideas for rewards and privileges from their students—and it's the surest way to choose positives that are meaningful to your middle-schoolers. But if you're looking for ideas to adapt to your kids, try these proven positives for rewarding individual students, classes, even your entire school.

Personalized Positives

Here are ways an individual teacher can reward individual students or the members of a cooperative group for good homework skills or appropriate behavior in class.

Second-Chance Report

Give a student whose record improves over the quarter for doing homework independently, or for turning it in on time, a chance to replace one grade by redoing an assignment. The work must demonstrate a clear improvement over the original to cancel the lower grade.

Coupon Mania

Clip store coupons for favorite teen snacks or coupons from teen magazines for inexpensive items young adolescents like, such as hair products and makeup. Store the coupons in a colorful box or basket. Let a student, or each member of a cooperative group, choose a coupon for appropriate behavior.

Freebies!

Coordinate with other staff members to obtain free passes to school sports activities; free lunches or free extras, like ice cream, in the cafeteria; free tickets to school plays or concerts, and so on. If possible, expand the incentives you can offer by enlisting community businesses or organizations to donate tickets to special events—such as a free pass to a hands-on science museum, a Saturday movie matinee, a local theater production, a fair or concert. When a student's behavior is exemplary, reward it with a freebie you know the student will enjoy.

For cooperative groups, your freebies will probably need to be less expensive. For example, you might treat each member to a snack from the cafeteria.

Special Duty

Arrange for students to perform such special duties as reading announcements over the school P.A. system, assisting in the office, or learning to use the school video camera and recording assemblies or other school events. This is where knowing students as individuals will help you determine what kind of activity will be best suited to a student's skills and most meaningful and exciting to him or her.

Team-Sponsored Rewards

Here are ways a team can reward appropriate behavior.

Privilege Pass

Award students who meet all behavior expectations for a week or a quarter with a "Privilege Pass" that gives them such privileges as permission to work in the library during study periods, use equipment in the computer lab during unscheduled periods or practice in the gym when it's not being used. Students must carry their Privilege Pass with them at all times. (For a page of ready-to-copy passes, see page 148.)

Privilege Pass

Duplicate the page on heavy paper for durability, cut apart individual passes, then be ready to present to students who team members agree demonstrate exemplary or greatly improved behavior. Note when the pass is issued and how long it is in effect. (You might give some students a probationary tryout, such as a week or month, before issuing a pass that's good for the semester or the year.) Post a list of privileges to which students are entitled in your classrooms and around the school.

Privilege PASS	**Privilege** PASS
Awarded to _____ for exemplary school behavior.	Awarded to _____ for exemplary school behavior.
Date _____	Date _____
Teacher's Name _____	Teacher's Name _____
Good for _____	Good for _____
Privilege PASS	**Privilege** PASS
Awarded to _____ for exemplary school behavior.	Awarded to _____ for exemplary school behavior.
Date _____	Date _____
Teacher's Name _____	Teacher's Name _____
Good for _____	Good for _____
Privilege PASS	**Privilege** PASS
Awarded to _____ for exemplary school behavior.	Awarded to _____ for exemplary school behavior.
Date _____	Date _____
Teacher's Name _____	Teacher's Name _____
Good for _____	Good for _____

Go for the Goal!

Challenge individual students to meet a particular behavior expectation in each class for a period of a day or a week. For example, set a goal of turning in all homework on time or following all directions in all classes. In exchange, the student receives a particular reward (a freebie, coupon to the school store, no homework over the weekend) which is administered by the team or the principal. State the goal and reward on a short-term behavior contract, and provide a place for the student and each teacher to sign. At the end of the day or week, the student takes the sheet to each teacher, who evaluates the student's behavior and signs the sheet if he or she agrees the student has met the goal.

Announcing Good Behavior

As a team, design an announcement or ad to appear in your school newspaper or on a school cable channel, which publicly congratulates your students for exemplary class behavior this quarter, improved academic work, or outstanding demonstration of cooperation and teamwork on a culminating unit activity. Be sure to identify each student, and let kids know in advance to watch for a special announcement coming soon. If your school cable channel can be accessed throughout your community, alert parents to the time and date of your broadcast.

We're a Winning Team!

Design a T-shirt with your team name, grade, school, and the school or team logo or mascot. (If you don't have one, invite students to submit entries for a "Name Our Team" or "Create a Team Logo" contest.) If you lack funds, enlist a local business to underwrite the cost of creating team T-shirts. Then award shirts to students for exemplary behavior or grades. (Aim to reward each student with a T-shirt by the end of the semester.) Plan a day when everyone, including teachers, wears the team T-shirts.

Class Positives

Try these ideas to reward a class for appropriate behavior.

Tally Ho!

Harness positive peer pressure by rewarding the class for individual effort. Set a goal—50 points—and a reasonable time period for achieving it. Then each time a student demonstrates appropriate behavior, score a point for the class. You can also offer challenges to the class: *"Everyone who brings in his or her homework completed and on time will score a point for the class. If you all make it, that will put us over the top and you'll get your reward—no homework tomorrow night!"* Other class rewards might include a movie on videotape, a free period for study and quiet talk, a pizza party, or special requests from the class.

Get-Down-to-Business Bonus

Announce to students that each time every student is on time, seated and ready to get down to business when the class begins, they're eligible for a class reward. Make sure students understand the rules: They don't receive a bonus every time, but when they least expect it, they'll get five minutes at the end of the period to talk, a chance to listen to music (let kids choose the tunes but you control the volume), no homework, or a reward of their own choosing. Note in your plan book each time students meet the get-down-to-business requirement. Let students know how many "bonuses" they've accumulated, and be sure to surprise them with a reward now and then to maintain their motivation.

The Chapter-a-Day Incentive

Here's a way to reward students and to introduce them to authors of young-adult books they might read on their own. Identify a problem that's shared by much of the class, such as not following directions, talking out of turn, moving around the classroom without permission, not completing homework and so on. Then offer the class a challenge: For each day the class meets your behavior or homework objective, you'll end the period by reading aloud a chapter from a young-adult novel. Let students choose the book from among a selection that appeals to boys as well as girls, such as *The Contender* by Robert Lipsyte, *Hatchet* by Gary Paulsen and *Maniac Magee* by Jerry Spinelli.

Schoolwide Positives

Here are ways to get all staff members involved in rewarding students for positive behavior, as well as ideas for motivating students to work together to create a positive school environment.

Gotcha! Gold Card

Be on the alert for students behaving appropriately! Have every staff member carry a pocket of "Gotcha! Gold Cards" to award students in the hall, in the cafeteria, outside on school grounds—anywhere they see kids following school rules, helping others

Gotcha! Gold Card

Gotcha! Catch students being good and reward them with a Gold Card. Students won't want to leave school without receiving one (or several)! Present these to any student any staff member sees following school rules, helping others and generally acting as a behavior role model. Set up a plan whereby students can redeem cards for privileges, prizes or other meaningful rewards.

Gotcha!	*Gotcha!*
Awarded to _____ For_____ By_____ Date _____ ⭐ GOLD CARD ⭐	Awarded to _____ For_____ By_____ Date _____ ⭐ GOLD CARD ⭐
Gotcha!	*Gotcha!*
Awarded to _____ For_____ By_____ Date _____ ⭐ GOLD CARD ⭐	Awarded to _____ For_____ By_____ Date _____ ⭐ GOLD CARD ⭐
Gotcha!	*Gotcha!*
Awarded to _____ For_____ By_____ Date _____ ⭐ GOLD CARD ⭐	Awarded to _____ For_____ By_____ Date _____ ⭐ GOLD CARD ⭐

and generally acting as a behavior role model. Post signs in the hallways that warn kids that "Gotcha!" means good behavior won't be overlooked. List items for which students can redeem a particular number of gold cards: 5 = a free lunch or extra from the cafeteria; 10 = school T-shirt or free period shooting baskets in the gym. Or plan a weekly raffle, where students can enter their Gotcha! cards toward a free meal at a local fast-food restaurant or a free CD or video from a local store. (For ready-to-reproduce Gotcha! Gold Cards, see page 149.)

Grading Your School

Here's a way to promote positive peer pressure and to involve all staff—from cooks, to bus drivers, to custodians—in encouraging appropriate student behavior. Set up a School Climate Committee of teachers, students, support staff and administrators to create a report card that identifies behaviors that the student body as a whole needs to improve. For example:

- Tardiness

- Truancy

- Littering on school grounds and in hallways and classrooms

- Discipline referrals to the office

- Behavior on the bus

- Inappropriate language

- Behavior in study hall

- Behavior in the hallways

- Behavior in the cafeteria

- Behavior on school grounds

Each staff member who agrees to participate is given a copy of the report card with a grade range, A–F, next to each behavior. Each week, staff members grade students to show improvement, no improvement, or a decline in each area. Report

cards are collected and marks tallied by the Climate Committee members to arrive at a grade average for each category, and compiling those averages, for the school overall. For each week there's improvement from the previous week, the student body receives one letter in the words SUPER STUDENTS or other meaningful phrase, which is posted on a sign outdoors or in a main hallway. Once all of the letters in the phrase have been earned, all students receive a reward, such as a free special meal at lunch or a free dance after school.

A Principal Feat

The key requirement for this idea is an administrator with a sense of humor! With your principal's agreement, issue the student body a behavioral challenge. If students meet a particular goal—such as 95 percent attendance for a month, fewer than four referrals to the office each week for the semester, no fights or suspensions for an entire semester—the principal agrees to an action or activity that will have special meaning for your students. Set up a system for recording students' progress toward the goal. If students meet the challenge, the entire student body gathers to watch the principal's "outrageous" feat—kissing a pig in public, taking a pie in the face, getting dunked in a tub of water, leading a team of teachers in a faculty-student game before the whole school. It's another opportunity to capitalize on school spirit and positive peer pressure to improve overall student behavior. And as schools that have tried similar "principal challenges" will testify, it can be a lot of fun!

Privilege Pass

Duplicate the page on heavy paper for durability, cut apart individual passes, then be ready to present to students who team members agree demonstrate exemplary or greatly improved behavior. Note when the pass is issued and how long it is in effect. (You might give some students a probationary tryout, such as a week or month, before issuing a pass that's good for the semester or the year.) Post a list of privileges to which students are entitled in your classrooms and around the school.

Privilege PASS

Awarded to _____
for exemplary school behavior.

Date _____

Teacher's Name_____

Good for_____

Privilege PASS

Awarded to _____
for exemplary school behavior.

Date _____

Teacher's Name_____

Good for_____

Privilege PASS

Awarded to _____
for exemplary school behavior.

Date _____

Teacher's Name_____

Good for_____

Privilege PASS

Awarded to _____
for exemplary school behavior.

Date _____

Teacher's Name_____

Good for_____

Privilege PASS

Awarded to _____
for exemplary school behavior.

Date _____

Teacher's Name_____

Good for_____

Privilege PASS

Awarded to _____
for exemplary school behavior.

Date _____

Teacher's Name_____

Good for_____

Gotcha! Gold Card

Gotcha! Catch students being good and reward them with a Gold Card. Students won't want to leave school without receiving one (or several)! Present these to any student any staff member sees following school rules, helping others and generally acting as a behavior role model. Set up a plan whereby students can redeem cards for privileges, prizes or other meaningful rewards.

Gotcha!

Awarded to _____

For _____

By _____

Date _____

★ G O L D   C A R D ★

Gotcha!

Awarded to _____

For _____

By _____

Date _____

★ G O L D   C A R D ★

Gotcha!

Awarded to _____

For _____

By _____

Date _____

★ G O L D   C A R D ★

Gotcha!

Awarded to _____

For _____

By _____

Date _____

★ G O L D   C A R D ★

Gotcha!

Awarded to _____

For _____

By _____

Date _____

★ G O L D   C A R D ★

Gotcha!

Awarded to _____

For _____

By _____

Date _____

★ G O L D   C A R D ★